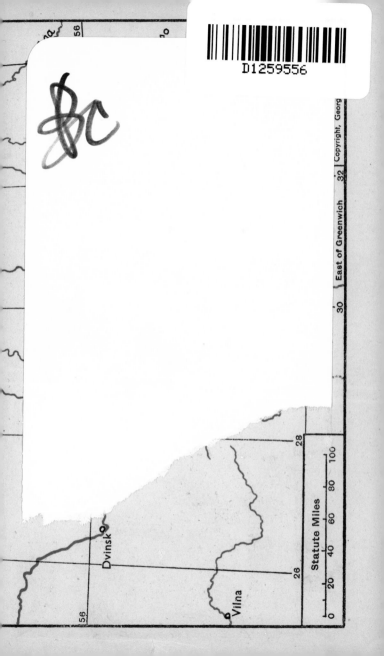

$8C

56

56

East of Greenwich

32 Copyright, Georg

30

28

26

Statute Miles

100

80

60

40

20

0

Dvinsk

Vilna

PUSHKIN

and

Russian Literature

is one of the volumes
in the

TEACH YOURSELF HISTORY
LIBRARY

Edited by A. L. ROWSE

Teach Yourself History

ALEXANDER S. PUSHKIN

PUSHKIN

and

Russian Literature

by
JANKO LAVRIN

Published by
HODDER & STOUGHTON LIMITED
for THE ENGLISH UNIVERSITIES PRESS
AT SAINT PAUL'S HOUSE
IN THE CITY OF LONDON

FIRST PRINTED   1947

PRINTED IN GREAT BRITAIN FOR THE ENGLISH UNIVERSITIES PRESS, LTD.,
LONDON, BY HAZELL, WATSON AND VINEY, LTD., LONDON AND AYLESBURY

A General Introduction to the Series

THIS series has been undertaken in the conviction that there can be no subject of study more important than history. Great as have been the conquests of natural science in our time —such that many think of ours as a scientific age *par excellence*—it is even more urgent and necessary that advances should· be made in the social sciences, if we are to gain control of the forces of nature loosed upon us. The bed out of which all the social sciences spring is history; there they find, in greater or lesser degree, subject-matter and material, verification or contradiction.

There is no end to what we can learn from history, if only we would, for it is coterminous with life. Its special field is the life of man in society, and at every point we can learn vicariously from the experience of others before us in history.

To take one point only—the understanding of politics: how can we hope to understand the world of affairs around us if we do not know how it came to be what it is? How to understand Germany, or Soviet Russia, or the United States —or ourselves, without knowing something of their history?

v

There is no subject that is more useful, or indeed indispensable.

Some evidence of the growing awareness of this may be seen in the immense increase in the interest of the reading public in history, and the much larger place the subject has come to take in education in our time.

This series has been planned to meet the needs and demands of a very wide public and of education—they are indeed the same. I am convinced that the most congenial, as well as the most concrete and practical, approach to history is the biographical, through the lives of the great men whose actions have been so much part of history, and whose careers in turn have been so moulded and formed by events.

The key-idea of this series, and what distinguishes it from any other that has appeared, is the intention by way of a biography of a great man to open up a significant historical theme; for example, Cromwell and the Puritan Revolution, or Lenin and the Russian Revolution.

My hope is, in the end, as the series fills out and completes itself, by a sufficient number of biographies to cover whole periods and subjects in that way. To give you the history of the United States, for example, or the British Empire or France, *via* a number of biographies of their leading historical figures.

That should be something new, as well as convenient and practical, in education.

I need hardly say that I am a strong believer in people with good academic standards writing once more for the general reading public, and of the public being given the best that the universities can provide. From this point of view this series is intended to bring the university into the homes of the people.

A. L. ROWSE.

ALL SOULS COLLEGE,
OXFORD.

Note

THIS study is not so much a biography as an attempt to present to a foreign audience a great literary figure through his own creations and against the background of the epoch in which he lived. Special attention has been paid to Pushkin as the most vital link between Russian and English literature. Fully aware of the size of the task, I had to limit myself to the essentials, leaving out several aspects which could be tackled only in a work of a much larger size.

As for the quotations, they are taken from the following publications:

(1) *Pushkin's Poems*, a selection translated by Walter Morison, published by Allen and Unwin for the Prague Press (pp. 31–32, 32–33, 39–40, 41–42, 46, 47, 49, 53, 57–58, 69–71, 72, 78–79, 104–105, 105–106, 215). Unpublished translations by the same hand appear on pp. 30–31, 51, 60–61, 68–69, 82–83, 100–101.

(2) *The Works of Alexander Pushkin*, edited by Avram Yarmolinsky (pp. 98, 101–102, 108–109), The translation of the quoted poems is by Babette Deutsch, Nonesuch Press, London, and Random House, N.Y.

(3) *Verse from Pushkin and Others*, translated by

Oliver Elton, published by Arnold (pp. 111–112, 113, 116).

(4) *A Book of Russian Verse*, edited by C. M. Bowra. Macmillan, 1843. The poem taken from it is on p. 99. The translation is by R. M. Hewitt, who also translated the poem on p. 100.

(5) For all the quotations from *Onegin* I am indebted to Oliver Elton's version of *Evgeny Onegin*, published by the Pushkin Press.

(6) Passages quoted in Chapter Eight are taken from *Little Tragedies*, translated by V. de S. Pinto and W. H. Marshall, published by the New Europe Publishing Company. Those from *Mozart and Salieri* are in R. M. Hewitt's translation (privately printed).

(7) The prose passage in Chapter Nine is from *The Captain's Daughter and Other Tales*, translated by Natalie Duddington (Everyman).

(8) The scene from *Boris Godunov* in Chapter Seven was specially translated for this book by V. de S. Pinto and W. H. Marshall.

My thanks and acknowledgments are due to the publishers and the translators of the works mentioned.

J. L.

Contents

Contents

Chapter One

Russia and her Literature before Pushkin

I

THE study of any literature, if undertaken in the right spirit, should enable us to follow the successive patterns of the life and consciousness of the nation which gave it birth. And since patterns of this kind are closely intertwined with economic, social and political factors, such a task can hardly be undertaken without an examination of the historical background of the nation or the country concerned. This is particularly true of Russian literature, the character of which can only be explained by the vagaries of Russian history from the days when the Russians, by becoming Christians, joined the comity of European nations. Yet the fact that the old Russia, with Kiev as its centre, received Christianity not from Rome but from the neighbouring Byzantium, with whom she had lively commercial contacts, created a cultural gap between Russia and Western Europe. Nor was it without significance that Kievian Russia, which became Christian only towards the end of the tenth century, received its first religious books from outside, namely from the Balkans, and in the language of the Balkan Slavs—a language akin to but not identical with Russian. A modified ninth-century Macedonian dialect was thus adopted by the Russians for liturgical purposes, and this Church-Slavonic tongue, as it is usually called, remained for centuries also the language of Russian literature, whose authors were for a long time chiefly monks and representatives of the higher clergy. The *Chronicle* of early Slav and Russian history attributed to the monk Nestor (*c.* 1056–1114) is one of the lasting monuments of the Kiev period of literature. A second and slightly later monument (from the end of the twelfth century) is *The Lay of Igor's Raid*, describing Prince Igor's expedition against the Mongolian Polovtsy, his defeat, captivity and final escape.[1]

Owing to her geographical position the Russia of that period was exposed to continuous incursions and invasions on the part of nomadic tribes coming from Asia. In the middle of the thirteenth century she at last fell a prey to the Tartars, and this catastrophe widened the gap between Europe and Russia. The Tartar dominion, which lasted some 250 years, not only stopped the promising cultural development of Kievian Russia, but erected an impassable barrier between her and the West at a time when the mighty wave of the Renais-

[1] Borodin's famous opera, *Prince Igor*, is based on this old work.

sance was already gathering momentum. If the chief function of the Renaissance was to secularise culture, i.e. to separate it (as far as possible) from theology and the Church, its parallel task was to emancipate the individual, intellectually and politically, from the fetters bequeathed to Europe by the feudal Middle Ages. The rise of national literatures, written in the spoken language and accessible to an increasing number of readers, was a natural result of this double tendency, the impetus of which was fostered by the newly invented art of printing. But Russia was debarred from all this. While the Western nations were forging ahead she remained for a long time practically untouched either by the Renaissance or by the Reformation. In such circumstances her creative genius asserted itself not so much in literature as in ecclesiastical architecture and religious art on the one hand and in an astonishingly rich folklore on the other.

Meanwhile the centre of Russian life had gradually shifted from the south to the safer central regions. When in the fourteenth century the metropolitan see was transferred from Vladimir to Moscow, the prestige of this city gained ground. In 1480 Ivan III, the Grand Duke of Muscovy, refused to pay the usual tribute to the Golden Horde, freed Russia from the Tartar yoke, and thus inaugurated the Moscow period of history and culture. But even when the Tartars had gone there was no immediate scope for

3

literary or cultural activities. The first task was
to consolidate the "gathered" Russian provinces.
In the circumstances such a task often required
ruthless measures, and the spirit which underlay
the autocratic regime of Moscow was duly reflected in the Church. Moreover, after the fall
of Constantinople Moscow began to regard herself as the "third Rome" and the only pivot of
true Christianity—an attitude which threatened
to erect a new barrier against the "heretical"
West. The feeble echoes of learning that trickled
now and then from Europe into Russia were
looked upon with suspicion. The cultural level
of the masses was so low that when in the second
half of the sixteenth century the first printing-
press was installed in Moscow, the printers were
driven out of the "third Rome" by the populace
like black magicians or hirelings of the devil.
But a change was bound to come, and come it did.

II

Certain contacts between Russia and Europe
were made by Ivan III (1440–1505) when he
married Sophia Paleologus, a niece of the last
Emperor of Byzantium. Half-Italian by birth
and by education, she took with her to Moscow
a number of Italian artisans and builders, including the Milanese architect Ridolfo di Fioravante,
who was responsible for the Assumption Cathedral
(subsequently used for the coronation of the Tsars)

in the Kremlin. Much of the Kremlin was built by the Italians. Hence its curious mingling of styles. Further progress in relations with the West was noticeable under Ivan IV (1530–84), better known as Ivan the Terrible, who, incidentally, was the first Grand Duke to assume the title of Tsar. A ruthless despot and a shrewd statesman, he saw that one of Russia's vital needs was an outlet to the Baltic. His ventures in this direction ended in failure, but his attempts to expand the territory of Russia towards the east and the south-east met with unqualified success. He conquered Kazan and Astrakhan on the Volga, and in 1581 added most of Siberia to his domain. Yet this was not enough to make Russia forget her interests in the West. Like Janus she had two faces: one turned towards the Asiatic East, and the other to Europe—a feature which remained typical of modern Russian history as a whole. Undaunted by his reverses in the Baltic region, Ivan the Terrible fostered a *rapprochement* with England. His Anglophilism was, with all its ups and downs, so persistent as to amount to Anglomania. But contacts came from the other side of the Baltic as well. In 1553 the English seaman Richard Chancellor landed on the North Russian coast, whence he proceeded to Moscow and was amicably received by the Tsar. A practical result of that journey was the foundation of the Muscovy Company for Trade with England. The Tsar granted it in 1556 a charter with all sorts

5

of privileges for the English merchants. Judging by his correspondence with Queen Elizabeth, he aimed at nothing less than an alliance between England and Russia. The cautious Elizabeth had to use all her tact in order to derive a maximum of commercial advantages with a minimum of political commitments. Nor was it an easy matter to dissuade that pious debauchee on the throne of Muscovy from marrying one of Queen Elizabeth's ladies and a distant relative—Mary Hastings.

Sympathy for England was maintained by Ivan's son-in-law, Boris Godunov (1552–1605), who eventually became Tsar.[1] A great coloniser of the Volga district and of Siberia, he was yet anxious to increase trade with England, and exempted the English merchants from tolls. He was also the first Muscovite ruler to send a few Russian youths abroad for purposes of education. Five of them went to England; but once having tasted English freedom none of them wished to return. During the "times of trouble" (at the end of the sixteenth and the beginning of the seventeenth centuries) Russia was in the throes of chaos and anarchy, which came to an end only after the election of the first Romanov to the throne in 1613. Under the Romanov dynasty the commercial and the cultural contacts with

[1] He promulgated in 1587 the ukase forbidding the peasants to move from one landowner to another, and this law was the actual foundation of serfdom in its worst form, which from now on weighed heavily upon Russia for nearly three hundred years.

the West were on the increase. Moscow by then had a large foreign quarter in which Western manners and ways of life prevailed. One of its denizens, the German pastor Gregori, founded in 1672 the first Russian theatre (or, to be exact, Court theatre) after the Western pattern. Tsar Alexis watched with childlike glee the clumsily translated plays, among which there was also a mutilated version (turned into Russian from a bad German translation) of Marlowe's *Tamburlaine*. Another interesting curiosity is the fact that the first person to collect Russian historical folksongs was the Oxonian Richard James who, acting as chaplain to the English Embassy, stayed in Russia during 1618–20.

An event of great importance took place in 1667, when the Ukraine east of the Dnieper was ceded by Poland to Russia. The same Kiev which once upon a time had received Christianity from Byzantium now served as an intermediary between Moscow and Western culture, the echoes of which reached the Ukraine via Poland. The first author of biblical plays (after the manner of the Jesuit school-plays) in Russian was the monk Simeon Polotsky (1629–80), who had studied in Kiev. A number of other belated Western influences and motives began to penetrate into Russian literature by the same channel, but without any spectacular results. Apart from such an isolated work of merit as the autobiographical *Life of the Archpriest Avvakum* (c. 1673), Muscovy had nothing that could be compared with the remarkable achievements of Western literatures, including that of Poland. Besides, her medium was still the dead Church-Slavonic language which had been imported into Kiev from the Balkans. In the best case an unsatisfactory mixture of Church-Slavonic and the spoken tongue was used. Things only became different after Peter the Great (1672–1725) had ascended the throne of Russia.

III

Of Russia's two faces—one turned towards Asia and the other towards Europe—Peter chose, and most resolutely, the second. Whereas his campaigns helped him to make Russia a part of civilised Europe, his reforms freed her from the weight of her "Asiatic" tradition. He travelled extensively abroad and stayed for longer periods in Great Britain and Holland, all the time anxiously studying everything that might be of use at home. His own education had been hasty and superficial, but he made up for it by his virile enthusiasm for enlightenment, which he did not hesitate to impose upon his country by unenlightened methods when necessary. Among his helpers there were, curiously enough, quite a few Scots: James Bruce, for example, Patrick Gordon, and the Tsar's personal physician Dr. Robert Erskine. It is true that by his short cuts, designed to yield a maximum of results within a limited time, Peter showed a keener sense for the practical, utilitarian side of life than for disinterested cultural values. Manuals of all sorts were translated and compiled. Scientists and technicians came in hundreds from the more advanced European countries. Feverish activities spread all over Russia, which now seemed to be in a hurry to redeem her stagnant past. To crown it all, Peter built his new capital, St. Petersburg, on the periphery of his State as a "window looking into Europe."

All these efforts were rounded off by his territorial adjustments and additions, among which those on the Baltic coast actually completed the task formerly aimed at by Ivan the Terrible. Having thus shifted Russia to the West, Peter put an end to the Moscow period of Russian history and opened up the new Petersburg period in the teeth of great opposition. In his ambition to secularise Russian culture he abolished the patriarchate and turned the Russian Orthodox Church itself into a department of the civil service. The only institution he left untouched was serfdom, which remained as evil as before, since serfs could be bought and sold like cattle. Nor did he do anything substantial to curtail the Russian autocratic system. So there was no guarantee that after his own enlightened despotism there would not arise, perhaps, some less enlightened despot who would try to undo most

9

of his work. Such despots did come after him, but fortunately it was no longer possible to put the clock back. After Peter the Great Russia could not but form a part of Europe, and Western influences became a vital factor in that fermentation through which she had to pass in order to realise not only her place but also her peculiar task in modern history.

The Petersburg period, which lasted from Peter the Great until the revolution of 1917, represents in its totality a rich and complicated achievement. It coincides, on the whole, with what is called modern literature proper, as distinct from the previous one in which the Church-Slavonic language prevailed. It was Peter the Great who simplified the Russian alphabet and made use of spoken Russian in his decrees, as well as in the first Russian newspaper which he founded in 1703 in Petersburg, himself becoming one of its principal contributors. He acted as a ploughman, furrowing the neglected soil and preparing it for the seed. And the sowers came soon after his death. In 1730 the not very successful poet V. K. Tredyakovsky laid down the rule that one should always write as one speaks. He made certain allowances for the use of Church-Slavonic archaisms only in the solemn ode and tragedy. Prince A. D. Kantemir (1708–44), who was Russian ambassador to Paris and London, was the first significant poet writing in spoken Russian and in the spirit of Petrine enlightenment. An

Anglophil and an admirer of Locke, he was also the first Russian poet to be introduced to Western Europe: a French translation (by Guasco) of his realistic-didactic satires appeared in London in 1749; that is, before they were published in the original.

Another and greater man who put Tredyakovsky's dictum about the spoken language into practice was Michael Lomonosov (1715–65). Having acquired the bulk of his knowledge in Germany, he became the first Russian scientist in a modern sense. But he was also a poet of odes and of anacreontic verse, a grammarian, and even something of a dramatist. It was Lomonosov who standardised the new literary language by adopting three styles according to the hierarchy of the *genres*. Whereas the lofty tragedy and ode could not entirely dispense with Church-Slavonic words and expressions, in the less solemn "middle style" of poetry the speech of the gentry came into its own. In comedy and the fable, on the other hand, the more common expressions used by the lower classes were allowed.

It stands to reason that only with the adoption of the spoken language could a national literature become possible, even if great results could not be accomplished overnight. Russia had first to learn from Europe advanced literary methods and technique, an apprenticeship which lasted until the end of the eighteenth century. A further difficulty was the absence of a proper reading-public. The peasant masses were illiterate. As for the gentry, Peter the Great had imposed upon them education of a sort, but its initial stages were bound to be poor and haphazard. Wealthy aristocrats, on the other hand, were content with the veneer of a French upbringing which often made them despise everything Russian, their native tongue included. It was only after Russia's continuous military successes against the Turks that her national consciousness began to grow and to take an interest not only in her warlike but in her cultural achievements as well.

IV

Anxious to adorn their country with a literature worthy of its military glory, Russian authors began by imitating French classical literature, the vogue of which swept over the whole of eighteenth-century Europe. Boileau was their law-giver. Tragedies in the style of Racine and Voltaire and comedies in the style of Molière were their ideal. Sumarokov, Ozerov and Knyazhnin provided more or less passable examples of the first, while Fonvizin wrote two sprightly comedies of manners in which the influence of Molière (and even more that of his Danish counterpart, Ludvig Holberg) was directed to Russian conditions with a great deal of realism and satire. The reading public was still much too small to turn literature into a paying proposition, but encouragement often came from the Court, particularly from that of Catherine II (1729–96).

Although a German by birth, that lewd but intelligent Empress continued, in her own way and for her own purposes, the work of Peter the Great. Surrounded by a galaxy of brilliant men, she encouraged both literature and enlightenment, at least as long as they suited her own ambitions. Her famous *Nakaz* or *Instructions* (1766), compiled mainly from Montesquieu's *L'esprit des lois* and from Beccaria, was so radically worded that its sale was forbidden in France. Her administrative abilities were of a high order, and her political horse-sense made her pay due attention to the interests of Russia in the West as well as in the East. While in the West she benefited from the partition of Poland, her able generals conquered from Turkey the whole of the Crimea with large stretches of the Black Sea coast—a feat which gave a new complexion to the Eastern problem. Amid all her activities she kept up a lively and witty correspondence with *les philosophes*, especially with Voltaire, d'Alembert and Diderot. At the same time it was during her rule that Anglophilism made big strides in Russia, but this itself was a reflection of the Anglomania then fashionable in France. Catherine also fostered the literature of her adopted country not only as a patron but as an authoress and a frequent contributor to the first satirical Russian magazine, *Pêle-mêle* (1769), modelled on

Addison's *Spectator*.[1] For a time, at any rate, the Court became the centre of Russian letters, and in some cases there was no sharp dividing-line between author and courtier. There was a good deal of the courtier even in the greatest Russian poet of that period, Gavrilo Derzhavin (1743–1816).

Derzhavin represents the apex of the pseudo-classic trend in Russian poetry. Brimming over with "Tartar" vitality, he often paid scant attention to poetic rules and even to those of grammar, but there is no denying that at his best he was really great. His magnificent sense of colour, combined with a temperamental and grandiosely rhetorical sweep, was responsible for the vogue his poems enjoyed at home and to some extent abroad: his *Ode to God*, for example, was translated into a score of languages, including Chinese.[2] But while the classical trend represented by Derzhavin was still fairly strong, N. M. Karamzin (1765–1826) introduced the so-called sentimental current into Russia. His *Letters of a Russian Traveller* created a sensation in the last decade of the eighteenth century. This follower of Rousseau and of the English senti-

[1] English literary influences in eighteenth-century Russia began with the journals in which there were plenty of borrowings, translations and adaptations from the *Spectator*. But when the Masonic humanitarian Novikov dared, in his own periodicals (*The Idler*, *The Painter*, *The Purse*), to satirise serfdom, they were quickly suppressed.

[2] In Great Britain, Derzhavin found a versatile translator in Sir John Bowring, whose *Specimens of the Russian Poets* appeared in 1821.

14

mentalists (especially of Richardson and Sterne) not only gave a varied and emotionally coloured account of his journey through Germany, Switzerland, France and England, but wrote in such polished prose as to become an idol of the younger generation. His tearful narrative *Poor Liza* was the most-read story of that period. After a number of other stories, poems and essays he settled down as an historian in order to produce, during the last twenty years of his life, the first monumental history of Russia or—as he called it—of the Russian State, written in a patriarchally conservative spirit.

But even before the one-time Rousseauist and enthusiast for freedom made this *volte-face*, Russian literature could boast of her first martyr in the person of A. Radishchev. Unaware of the fact that because of the excesses of the French revolution Catherine had without warning shed all her zest for enlightenment, Radishchev published in 1790 a work under the modest title *A Journey from Petersburg to Moscow*. The book was modelled on Sterne's *Sentimental Journey*, but lacked its lightness of touch. Radishchev's prose was heavy, often long-winded; what mattered, however, was the contents of the book, which consisted for the most part of a merciless criticism of Russian life—in the spirit of the same enlightenment which a quarter of a century earlier Catherine herself had endorsed in her *Nakaz*. The author was so outspoken about serfdom (and by

15

implication also about autocracy) that Catherine,
furious at his temerity, sentenced him to death.
This sentence was commuted to exile in Siberia,
where Radishchev remained until 1796, when
Catherine died.

The rupture between the Court and literature
thus took a dramatic turn, although it was not
yet final. Neither Karamzin nor his follower
V. Zhukovsky was in opposition to the Court.
Besides, the sentimental trend so dear to both,
with its resigned faith in a guiding Providence,
fully coincided with the moods of their patron
Alexander I. In spite of this, from Karamzin
onwards the guardianship of literature began to
pass to the educated representatives of the gentry.
Karamzin himself carried the language-reform a
stage farther by reducing Lomonosov's three
styles to the "middle style" alone. The standardised speech of the gentry thus became the un-
disputed literary language of Russia. Braving
a few die-hard archaists such as Admiral Shishkov,
the two principal younger poets, V. Zhukovsky [1]
and the neo-classicist, K. Batyushkov, followed
in the footsteps of Karamzin and did such
excellent work as to pave the way for Pushkin,
that central figure and in many respects founder
of Russian national literature.

[1] The meditative and sentimental romanticist Zhukovsky
rendered enormous services to Russian literature by his translations from other European literatures. It was he who in
1802 gave a superb translation of Gray's *Elegy* and in 1821
introduced Byron to Russian readers by his no less excellent
version of *The Prisoner of Chillon*.

V

If Peter I "annexed" Russia to Europe and at the same time turned her into a Great Power, Alexander Sergeyevich Pushkin (1799-1837) achieved, just over a century later, something similar with regard to Russian literature and, for that matter, Russian culture in general. There was in fact a certain affinity between these two geniuses. Pushkin, like Peter the Great, typified the belated Renaissance spirit in Russia, while trying to make up—by a short cut, as it were— for her lost opportunities in the past. They resembled each other in their broadness, their assimilative power, their intuitive awareness of the *Zeitgeist*, as well as in their Russian character; for their cosmopolitan sympathies did not in the least interfere with what was essentially Russian in both. No wonder Pushkin felt curiously drawn towards a monarch whose work he admired precisely because he understood it in all its implications. "Peter was undoubtedly a revolutionary by God's grace," he wrote in 1836. "The tremendous revolution achieved by his autocratic power abolished the old system of life, and European influences spread all over Russia. Russia entered Europe like a launched ship, accompanied by the noise of axes and firing guns. . . . As the executioner of an era which no longer corresponded to the nation's needs, the

Tsar brought us culture and enlightenment, which in the end must bring us freedom also."

Pushkin could not but side with Peter the revolutionary, and for good reasons. As a member of that section of the gentry which was not on good terms either with the Court aristocracy or with the higher bureaucracy, he (like so many other younger members of his class) adhered to the advanced bourgeois-liberal opinions of his period, and therefore wanted to see Peter's work carried to its logical end. Peter, who in so drastic a manner set the whole of his country before the problem of Europe and Russia, also bequeathed to the younger generations the task of solving it. And there were only three ways in which it could be tackled. The first was Russia as a docile imitation of Europe. Russia asserting her own individuality against the encroaching Europe was the second. And the third was the prospect of an organic synthesis between the two. Each of these trends seems to have been tried out by Russia at some time or other in the course of her recent history. Hence her vagaries, experiments and contradictions, which are by no means over. Yet in Russian culture, at any rate, one can distinguish the third trend in the making. Russian music, for instance, represents a successful blending of European methods and traditions with Russian material and an essentially Russian spirit. The same

18

applies to modern Russian literature, the prodigious growth of which, during the last hundred years or so, has been to a large extent a continuation and at the same time a completion of the possibilities inaugurated by Pushkin's work.

Chapter Two

Pushkin and his Background

PUSHKIN was born in Moscow on May 26th (O.S.), 1799. He himself was fond of pointing to the six-hundred-years-old nobility of his ancestors, some of whom figure in the annals of Russian history. His parents were well-connected landowners whose habit of living beyond their means was hardly conducive to prosperity. There is no indication that Pushkin the boy was much attached to either of them. The only member of the family likely to impress him was his uncle, Vasily Pushkin, a minor poet known (or rather notorious) for his flippant and scarcely printable narrative in verse *A Dangerous Neighbour*. There was however one person in the Pushkin household who exercised a lasting influence upon him: his nurse Arina Rodionovna. This peasant woman, whose sincere and simple affection meant so much to Pushkin, was the first link between him and the Russian people. Another factor of some importance was his father's French library, of which Pushkin as a boy made ample use, but without anybody's advice or guidance.

Thanks to his parents' connections he entered at the age of twelve the Lycée at Tsarskoye Selo (a privileged boarding-school opened by Tsar Alexander on October 19th, 1811) and remained there until June 1817, during which time some of the most exciting events in modern Russian history took place. It should be remembered that only two years after Pushkin's birth the half-mad Emperor Paul I—the "Russian Caligula," as Pushkin later called him—was "liquidated" in a palace-revolution led by Count Pahlen. His son Alexander I, who is supposed to have been connected with the murder, ascended the throne with a halo of goodwill and full of liberal intentions. There was even a time when he flirted with the idea of abolishing serfdom. But though this plan came to nothing, the new Tsar was responsible for several reforms in administration as well as in education, both higher and elementary. Besides other colleges, the Universities of Kharkov and Kazan were founded during his rule. So was the famous public library at St. Petersburg, one of the biggest in the world. Periodicals, too, were increasing in quantity and quality. A proper reading-public, small though it was at first, made its appearance, and there was a pathetic thirst for knowledge among the younger representatives of the gentry. All this was accompanied by a series of political and military happenings the climax of which was reached during the Napoleonic wars.

The conflict between Alexander and Napoleon, which had loomed on the horizon, became by

1804 unavoidable. The execution of the Duke
of Enghien only made matters worse. Nor was
Napoleon's assumption of the title of "Emperor"
to the Tsar's taste. A closer *rapprochement* between
Russia, Great Britain and Austria was sub-
stantiated by Alexander's military help to his
Austrian partner. But this only resulted in a
number of defeats, the most humiliating of which
was that at Austerlitz on November 20th, 1805.
The peace of Tilsit that followed was a com-
promise-peace which could not last. New misunderstandings arose and came to a head in 1812,
when Napoleon invaded Russian territory and
thus precipitated his own doom. However
patiently Russia had watched and waited while
her soldiers were campaigning abroad, the issues
became different after Napoleon's polyglot army
had crossed her frontiers. As though by a miracle
the nation awoke to the danger, which was acute
enough to sweep the whole population, from the
aristocrats to the humblest serfs, in one powerful
wave of patriotism. The burning of Moscow and
the rout of Napoleon's army increased the elation
throughout the country. Russia's leading rôle
in the coalition against Napoleon; the Tsar and
his armies in Paris; their triumphant return
home in 1815—all this could not but fill the
Russians with pride and hopeful expectations.
The more so because many a young officer who had
been as far as Paris came back anxious to apply his
conception of Western progress to his own country.

Yet there was a dark side to it. Flushed by his victories, by his easy personal triumphs in Vienna (during the Congress days) and in Paris, Tsar Alexander—an amiable weakling without stamina or independence of mind—began to regard himself as a higher being chosen by Destiny to rescue his own country, as well as the rest of Europe, from the clutches of revolutionary ideas. This was particularly the case after the formation of a Holy Alliance between Russia, Austria and Prussia for the purpose of upholding reaction at home and abroad. Instead of continuing his reforms the Tsar preferred to dabble in the spurious second-hand mysticism which was the fashion of the day. After a generation fed on Voltaire and *les philosophes*, the writings of Jung-Stilling were now read; the Catholic author Joseph de Maistre was a great favourite with Petersburg society, and some of the Jesuit schools were patronised by the best Russian families. The sentimental religious charlatan, the authoress Mme Kruedener, was (for a time at least) on the friendliest terms with Alexander himself.

While this wave of cant, sham-piety and "mystical" exaltation was getting hold of the Court and of those connected with it, the country was at the mercy of Arakcheyev—one of the stupidest and cruellest martinets modern Russia has known. Instead of a new life as the outcome of all the sacrifices during the Napoleonic wars, there was only a new triumph of despotism, at a

23

time when the economic position of Russia (as a result of prolonged wars) was far from satisfactory. Sporadic riots among the serfs did not bode anything good either. But discontent was also growing among the more intelligent members of the upper classes,. with the increase of secret or semi-secret societies as its obvious result.

II

The ground for such societies had been prepared by the strong Masonic movement in post-Petrine Russia. According to the literary historian A. N. Pypin, during the century between Peter the Great and Alexander I there had been in Russia 187 Masonic lodges of all kinds. The transition to societies with a definite liberal political colouring was thus made easier, especially among the officers who had taken part in the campaign of 1812. Cosmopolitan in their outlook but patriotic in their feelings, some of these officers formed in 1817 the "League of Salvation or of the True and Faithful Sons of the Fatherland." A year later it was given the less solemn title of the "Welfare League." Inspired by active idealism, its founders dreamed of abolishing serfdom and of turning Russia into a constitutional State. The League became definitely an underground movement in 1822, after all societies—Masonic or otherwise—had been forbidden. Gradually it was divided into the more

24

moderate Northern Society, with its seat in Petersburg, and the radical Southern Society (led by Colonel Pestel) whose centre was the distant Ukrainian town of Tulchin. In 1825 the "League of the United Slavs" was added to it. This was in touch with dissatisfied Polish patriots, and some of its members went so far as to theorise about a vague republican federation of the liberated Slavs in general. With the growth of "Arakcheyevism" the aims of both societies took on an increasingly militant colouring, and their ringleaders did not shrink from the idea of a rising if a change of regime in Russia should become imperative.

Unpractical and badly organised, the conspirators waited for their chance, which came soon enough. After the Tsar's death (in November 1825) Alexander's brother, Constantine, was to succeed him, but he abdicated in favour of his younger and not very popular brother Nicholas. The three weeks of tension which followed Constantine's abdication were regarded by the Northern Society as favourable for a revolt. But an armed revolt was impossible without the soldiers, who had not—and indeed could not have—a clear idea of what it was all about. As these had already taken the oath to Constantine, it was first necessary to convince them that the demand of a new oath to the much-hated disciplinarian Nicholas was a betrayal, not only of the rightful heir to the throne, but also of the soldiers' interests. So on December 14th (O.S.), 1825, the rebel officers marched together with their units to the Senate Square. Some of the soldiers who clamoured for Constantine and the Constitution were convinced that Constitution (in Russian, *konstitutsia*) was Constantine's wife, but this made little difference. Having refused to disperse, they were attacked, and the revolt came to an end in no time. Nicholas took a cruel revenge. Five ringleaders—among them the spirited civic poet K. Ryleyev—were hanged. The other "Decembrists," as they were henceforth called—120 in all—were sent to Siberia, there to expiate their dreams of a better and happier Russia.

Nicholas I had inherited the mentality of the Holy Alliance, but in contrast to the sentimental and vacillating Alexander I he was made all of a piece. Not devoid of personal charm, of which (like an actor) he was fully aware, he believed in autocracy, reaction and military discipline. These he practised so consistently that his methods were bad even when his intentions happened to be good, or what he considered good. It was he who created the dreaded "Third Section" with the task of keeping a watchful eye on his subjects and tracking down any murmur of sedition. Even private correspondence could be interfered with in the name of law and order. The word "freedom" was banned from the vocabulary, and the Tsar's hatred of any disobedience was notorious.

He not only crushed the Polish rebellion in 1831 but offered to suppress the Hungarian rising in 1848–9, just for the sake of "principle"; and did so.

The "leaden" era of his rule was one of drab uniformity and of police regulations, while the bureaucratic system, notorious for its corruption, was accessible to all sorts of opportunists and place-hunters. In such a system there was hardly any room left for the honest and educated members of the gentry who in those days were the only upholders of progressive tendencies in Russia. Add to this the pitiful position of the serfs, whose liberation was shelved indefinitely as the rising price of corn in Europe seemed to have made serf-labour profitable once more. The state of affairs remained practically the same as towards the end of Alexander's rule, and in some respects it grew worse. The only bright spot in that gloomy picture was presented by the "Decembrists" and by the *élite* of the younger generation as a whole. It was here that the name of Pushkin emerged, soon to become one of the greatest in his country.

III

Pushkin was fortunate to find in the Lycée where he studied congenial comrades and even some truly enlightened teachers. Although a bad pupil from the outset, he liked the general atmosphere which, among other things, encouraged his interest in literature. His exceptional poetic gift was at once acknowledged by his school-fellows, and his Lycée verses were popular among them. Pushkin's first printed poem, *To My Poet Friend*, appeared in 1814, in the April number of the well-known periodical *The European Messenger* (founded by Karamzin). Less than a year after, on January 8th, 1815, the aged poet Derzhavin was present at an examination during which Pushkin recited his own "Derzhavinesque" *Reminiscences in Tsarskoye Selo* with rather unexpected results for himself. This is how he describes the scene: "Derzhavin was very old. He was in uniform and wore his soft boots. Our exams tired him very much; he sat resting his chin on his hands; his face was expressionless, his eyes dull, and his lower lip drooping. He kept dozing, until the time came for questions on Russian literature. Then he suddenly woke up, his eyes sparkled, and he became a different man. His own poems were, of course, recited, analysed and repeatedly praised. He listened with unusual interest. At last my turn came. I read my *Reminiscences in Tsarskoye Selo*, only two steps away from Derzhavin. I cannot describe what it felt like. When I reached the passage in which I mention Derzhavin's name, my boyish voice rang clearly, and my heart began to thump as though I were in a state of intoxication. I do not remember how I finished my recital. Nor do I remember how I ran away. Derzhavin was enchanted. He wanted to see me, embrace me. They looked for me in vain."

Even before leaving the Lycée Pushkin was allowed to join the exclusive Arzamas Society founded in 1815 by Karamzin's followers— Zhukovsky, Batyushkov, Vyazemsky, etc.—in open defiance of the "archaists." The actual flowering of his original genius dates, however, from the summer of 1817, when he began his stay of nearly three years in St. Petersburg. Nominally, Pushkin became an official in the Ministry of Foreign Affairs, but he paid little or no attention to the performance of his duties. His only two occupations were poetry and pleasure, and pleasure often came first. Petersburg, with the memories of 1812 still lurking in the background, was full of life, and Pushkin plunged into his new experiences with reckless abandon, especially when in the congenial company which he rarely lacked. He was welcomed most of all in the "Green Lamp" circle formed in 1818 by young officers in the guards who were interested in literature, in liberal politics as well as in wine and pretty women. Full of vitality and gay malice, Pushkin scintillated among the "Green Lamp" members with his showers of caustic epigrams. These were all the more appreciated because of their frequent revolutionary flavour which made no secret of Pushkin's own political sympathies. While one part of his nature was still rooted as it were in the aristocratic eighteenth century, with its gallant eroticism and its cult of wit and gaiety, Pushkin was steeped in the bourgeois-liberal spirit of protest typical of the French Revolution as well as of the advanced minds of his generation. He expressed it plainly enough in his youthful *Ode to Liberty* (1817) in which he invoked that "dread of the Tsars"—the Muse of Revolution, and like a new Radishchev set out to "sing freedom to the world and crush the vice sitting on the throne." A homage to liberty was also the Epistle he addressed in 1818 to his philosophic friend P. Chaadayev. This is how he described in it the disappointment that befell his generation, which yet refused to submit to its ordeal:

Not long have we by love's sweet thrills,
By hope and fame been led astray.
Like smoke, like mist on morning hills,
    Young pleasures fade away.

But in our hearts desire still seethes:
Beneath oppression's fateful hand
Through our impatient souls there breathes
    The call of fatherland.

We long for freedom, and there burns
Within our hearts hope's sacred fire;
Just so a youthful lover yearns
    To gain his heart's desire.

While we respond to freedom's name,
While honour still moves heart and hand,

Let us devote our inner flame
    To this our fatherland.

Believe me, comrade, we shall see
The dawning of a joyful morn,
And Russia, from her slumbers torn,
The ruins of autocracy
    Will with our names adorn.

Such was the mood that animated the Decembrists during the political honeymoon of the Holy
Alliance. But Pushkin did not stop here. Aware
of all the abuses and iniquities, he vented in his
poem *In the Country* (1819) his disgust with what
he saw around. At the sight of the idyllic beauties
of Nature—far away from "Tsardom's courts,
sumptuous banqueting, vain pastimes," he mused:

Amidst these flowering fields and hills
The friend of man, appalled, perceives the trace
A shameful ignorance has stamped on every face.
    Blind to all tears, and deaf to every groan,
Chosen by destiny to ruin other lives,
Heartless and lawless, here a race of masters
        thrives;
    Wielding a ruthless rod, it makes its own
    The peasant's toil, his chattels and his days;
Behind a borrowed plough, obedient to the lash,
    Starved slaves the earth with furrows gash
    For lords whom no entreaty sways.
Here all bear heavy yokes till their last hours;
Afraid to nourish hope, or answer love's sweet call,
    The tender maiden flowers
To serve the lusts of some base criminal;
    Companion of his parents' toil and tears,

The son, the sweet support of their declining years,
  From the parental roof must hence
To swell the sorry crowd of lackeys at the hall.
  Oh, could my voice all hearts inspire!
  Why does my bosom burn with fruitless fire
  And my poor tongue lack burning eloquence?
Friends, shall I ever see my nation, freed, arise,
And serfdom vanish at a Tsar's command,
  And over freedom's fatherland
A lovely dawn illuminate the skies?

After his attack on autocracy, Pushkin in this poem struck a blow at Russia's second great evil: serfdom. But since autocracy and serfdom were the Siamese twins of the entire Russian system, he did not mind which of the two received the heavier blows. One was as good as the other. The main thing was to defend freedom, no matter what the pretext. When in March 1819 the German student Sand stabbed in Mannheim the notorious political spy in Russia's pay, Kotzebue (otherwise known as a popular German novelist and playwright), and was afterwards executed, Pushkin celebrated his deed as an act of justice in one of his most revolutionary poems, *The Dagger* (1821). Its first three verses are enough to give one an idea of the whole :

Thou secret punisher of Freedom's rape,
Dagger that dost the final judgment yield,
    For deathless Nemesis to wield
    A god on Lemnos gave thee shape.

Like dart from Hell, or bolt by gods released,
Thy silent blade gleams in the tyrant's eyes;
    He trembles, as around he spies
      For death amid the feast.

Where'er he be, thy point seeks out his sin:
On land, on sea, in temple, in the field,
    On passion's couch, amongst his kin,
      By secret locks concealed.

Pushkin valued his own creative freedom too much to commit himself, as his friend K. Ryleyev had done, to political or propaganda poetry. On the other hand, the propaganda value of his verses increased precisely because they were good as poetry. It goes without saying that poems of this kind could not appear in print; they circulated in written copies. Unfortunately Pushkin's *Ode to Liberty*, together with some biting epigrams against fools and scoundrels in high places, reached the police. Things began to look bad for him, but in the end it came to nothing worse than banishment to the South of Russia. He left St. Petersburg at the beginning of May 1820, only a few weeks before the appearance of a complete edition of his *Ruslan and Ludmila*.

IV

Pushkin first stopped at Ekaterinoslav (now Dniepropetrovsk). He was allowed to retain his post in the civil service and was lucky enough to find in his new chief, General Inzov, a lenient superior who never thought of interfering with his escapades unless these had gone too far. All things considered, his banishment was light, and in some respects a blessing in disguise. With few opportunities for wasting his time and energies he could now devote his leisure to writing and to extensive reading, as well as to travels, which he began immediately on his arrival in Ekaterinoslav. Falling ill, he was taken by General Rayevsky (one of the heroes of 1812) and his family to the Caucasus and then to Gurzouf in the Crimea, a journey which left an indelible stamp on Pushkin's work. Here, in the romantic Caucasus, he became acquainted with the poetry of Byron. At the same time the general's youngest daughter, Maria, kindled in him the flame of a romantic love which like a shadow pursued him for years. As his English was shaky he read most of Byron in French translations, while being helped by Maria's brother Nicholas to read him also in the original. The offshoot of it all was Pushkin's Byronic period, which proved of vital importance for his development.

It was Pushkin who created the first Byronic hero in Russia. An additional factor that brought Pushkin close to Byron was the Greek rising. In Kishinev, the capital of Bessarabia, whither he had followed his chief, Pushkin met a number of Greek refugees, including their one-armed leader Alexander Ypsilanti, and appreciated their eagerness to fight for liberty. On February 22nd, 1821, Ypsilanti made a crossing of the river Pruth and invaded Jassy, the capital of the province of Moldavia. The Greek leader was sure that the Tsar would support the rising against the Turks, but he was mistaken. Alexander I remained passive and actually seemed to disapprove of the Greek revolt, as though fearing lest its success might be followed by a series of revolts in other countries and thus contribute to the spread of sedition in Europe. Ypsilanti's failure was a disappointment for Pushkin, who must in the meantime have had some bitter personal experiences with "these new Leonidases," as he ironically called them in a letter. "I am neither a Barbarian nor an apostle of the Koran; the Greek cause interests me very much indeed; but for this very reason I am all the more indignant when I see these miserable fellows invested with the sacred office of defenders of freedom."

It stands to reason that the semi-Asiatic Kishinev was hardly a suitable place for gauging the struggle for freedom. On the other hand, its bohemian happy-go-lucky atmosphere appealed to one side of Pushkin's nature. It certainly provided scope for all sorts of bouts and scandals, to which he added a literary escapade by his *Gabriliada*, a parody on the Annunciation in Parny's lascivious manner. However excellently written, this poem is unworthy of Pushkin's

35

genius, even if its blasphemy (similar to that of a reckless schoolboy) may have been something of a protest against the "piety" and pseudo-mysticism radiating from the Court.[1] While in Bessarabia Pushkin visited Davidov's estate at Kamenka in the Ukraine, where he met several prospective Decembrists. His personal contact with them was thus maintained in the South, too.

In June 1823 Pushkin was transferred to Odessa, where the social and cultural level was higher than at Kishinev. Nevertheless his mode of life remained divided as before between poetry, wine and women. There were two women in particular who aroused in him, almost simultaneously, something stronger than a superficial attachment. Amalia Riznich, the beautiful Italian wife of a Serbian corn-merchant, was one of them. The other was Countess Vorontsov, the wife of the Governor-General of the province, Pushkin's immediate chief. Amalia was capable of stirring the poet's passion, as well as jealousy, to its highest pitch, if we are to judge by some of the verses he dedicated to her. The Countess, on the other hand, had a quiet charm of her own which was much enhanced by her intelligence. Pushkin paid due homage to both. No wonder that the Count, a cold, bureaucratic snob, took a dislike to the poet and did all he could to vex him. As the tension between the two increased, he was on the

[1] Pushkin's blasphemies were in no way directed against religion in a militant sense; they were rather an expression of his unusually strong tendency to joke and to parody.

look-out for some pretext to have Pushkin removed from Odessa altogether, and in the end
he found one. The police, on opening one of
Pushkin's private letters, discovered a passage
which could be interpreted as a proof of his
"atheism." Incensed at such a discovery, the
pious authorities thought it imperative to have
the poet sent to another place of exile—at a
respectable distance from Odessa. This time it
was his mother's estate, Mikhaylovskoye in the
district of Pskov. He set out in July 1824.

V

In this remote corner of northern Russia
Pushkin spent over two years: rather lonely but
on the whole the most creative years of his life.
And this in spite of his troubles, some of which
he described in the following letter to the poet
Zhukovsky (October 31st, 1824): "When I
arrived here I was well received by all, but things
soon changed. My father, shocked by my banishment, kept repeating all the time that the same
fate lay in store for him. Peshchurov,[1] who has
been entrusted with the task of supervising my
behaviour, was shameless enough to ask my
father to open my correspondence, that is, to
spy on me. My father's ill-temper and irritated
state of nerves precluded any talk with him; so
I decided to hold my tongue. He began reproach-

[1] The local marshal of nobility.

ing my brother for allowing me to teach him atheism. Still I remained silent. Then came the official report concerning my personal habits and ideas. I tried to extricate myself from the painful situation by going to my father and asking him whether I could speak to him frankly. He flew into a rage. I bowed, mounted my horse and went for a ride. He called my brother and forbade him to have anything more to do with *ce monstre, ce fils dénaturé*. Zhukovsky, imagine what my position is like and judge for yourself. Seething with indignation, I wanted to see my father; found him in mother's room and told him all I had been hiding in my heart during the last three months. In the end I declared I would never speak to him again. Taking advantage of the fact that no witnesses were present, my father rushed out of the room and told the entire household that I had struck him, had wanted to strike him, had raised my hand to strike him, might have struck him. My father's accusation is known to the entire household. No one believes it, yet they all gossip about it. The neighbours too have heard of it; but I do not want to have anything to do with them. Just imagine what will happen if the government hears of the matter. To put my father in court as a slanderer would be horrid. Besides, I am not entitled to have recourse to legal justice. I am *hors la loi*."

The outcome of it all was that Pushkin's father departed in a hurry, while he himself settled down to another two years of exile, at a time when his national fame as a poet was already established. It was at Mikhaylovskoye that he wrote some of his best lyrics, and continued to work at his masterpiece, *Evgeny Onegin*, which he had started in the South. Moreover, he had enough leisure to make a closer acquaintance with the works of Shakespeare, under whose influence he wrote his own historical play *Boris Godunov*.

The monotony of a country existence was partly relieved by his visits to Mme Osipova and her two daughters at the neighbouring estate of Trigorskoye. He also frequented country fairs, where he studied the simple folk and jotted down some of their songs and tales. Quite a few of these he heard from his old nurse, Arina, whose motherly care made his stay at Mikhaylovskoye more endurable. During the long winters Pushkin spent many an evening in her hut, the blizzard knocking on the windows and Arina dozing at her spinning-wheel. He recorded the nostalgia of those hours in his moving *Winter Evening*, which ends with these characteristic lines:

> Storm has wrapped the sky in darkness,
> Twists the snow in dances wild;
> Like a beast of prey it grumbles,
> Whimpers like a frightened child.
>
> Let us drink, then, old companion
> Of my youth so sad and drear;

Drown our sorrows; where's the beaker
That will fill our hearts with cheer?

Whatever the drawbacks of this compulsory
sojourn, it saved the poet from the *débâcle* of
December 14th. Had he been in Petersburg at
the time he would probably have taken part in
the revolt, although its ringleaders—reluctant to
make him run the same risk as they themselves—
abstained from initiating Pushkin into their plans
and intentions. Even so, his association with the
rebels was known to the police. Hand-written
copies of his seditious verses were found among
the papers of the arrested Decembrists, but since
he had not been on the scene of the actual revolt
no drastic measures could be taken against him.
Still, his fate was uncertain. Famous as a poet
and read all over Russia, he had yet nothing to
look forward to except a new series of suspicions
and vexations. But here a dramatic change took
place. What happened was nothing less than a
meeting with Tsar Nicholas I, who during the
coronation festivities in Moscow (in September
1826) suddenly remembered the exile and
despatched a special courier to bring him at once
for a personal interview. The order was duly
carried out. The Tsar and the poet met, and
this event led to a series of unforeseen conse-
quences in Pushkin's life.

Chapter Three

The Tsar and the Poet

I

WHEN at the age of twenty-seven Pushkin was summoned before the Tsar he knew that he had escaped only by a hair's breadth the fate of his rebel friends. At times he was inclined to see something miraculous in this escape, and aptly compared it with that of the ancient poet Arion, who on a sea-voyage was saved from death by reaching the shore on a dolphin's back. The poem in which Pushkin expressed his own relief once the storm was over actually bears the title *Arion*, and runs as follows:

> A varied crowd the vessel filled;
> And some the sheets were fast unfurling,
> Others united efforts hurling
> Against deep-plunging oars. When stilled
> Was all their tumult, and the rudder
> Answered the helmsman's cunning thrust,
> I, in my heart a carefree trust,
> Sang to the crew. A roaring gust
> Suddenly made the ocean shudder . . .
> The helmsman perished, and the crew;
> And me alone, who strange songs knew,
> The billows cast on friendly beaches.

My former hymns of praise sing I
While my wet clothes I spread to dry
Beneath a rock the sunshine reaches.

It must have been in such a mood that Pushkin, accompanied by the Tsar's courier, hurried from Mikhaylovskoye to Moscow. What exactly his interview with the Tsar was like and what the two men discussed when *tête-à-tête* can only be surmised from a few hints and rumours. The most interesting of these is the brief account given by Pushkin himself to a certain Mme Khomutova and printed in the periodical *Russian Archives* in 1867. According to it Pushkin was taken on his arrival, dressed as he was and still covered with mud, straight to the Emperor, who received him with informal cordiality. "The Emperor and I talked a great deal, and then he suddenly asked: 'Tell me, Pushkin, would you have taken part in the revolt on December 14th had you been in Petersburg?'—'Most certainly, Sire. All my friends were involved in the plot, and had I been there I could not have acted otherwise. My absence saved me, and God be thanked for it!'— 'Well, do not fool about any longer,' said the Emperor; 'I hope you'll be sensible from now on; there is no longer any need why we two should quarrel. Send me all your writings from now on: it is I who shall be your censor.'"

Nicholas meant what he said. Playing (like the consummate actor he was) at magnanimity, he probably cherished secret hopes that Pushkin's genius might be hitched to his reactionary policy and to the official conception of "law and order." If we are to believe the accounts of witnesses— one of them, written by A. P. Pyatkovsky, appeared in *Russian Antiquities* in 1880—the Tsar, on leaving his study together with Pushkin, pointed at the poet and said to those present: "From now on he is mine."

He was mistaken. Pushkin may have been beguiled at first by the Tsar's diplomatic charm, even to the extent of confessing in a poem his admiration for Nicholas. But instead of being converted to his policy he merely idealised him, until such time as fresh disappointments ensued. And they came soon enough—on both sides. Anxious to turn the "most remarkable man in Russia" (as Nicholas called Pushkin after the interview) into a sympathiser with the official regime, the Tsar was far from being reassured about the poet's political loyalties. Hence his magnanimous gesture with regard to the censorship. In volunteering to be the only censor of Pushkin's writings he intended to muzzle him beforehand through feigned generosity, knowing full well that the poet would carefully weigh each word before submitting it to such an exalted judge. As though to test him, Nicholas asked Pushkin soon after the interview to send him in a special memorandum his ideas about education in Russia. Pushkin accepted the challenge, and expressed his thoughts on the subject with such frankness as

to justify the Tsar's suspicions. The august reply,
graciously transmitted to Pushkin, was to the
effect that his views on education were a "menace
to general tranquillity," and that "good morals
and zealous service are preferable to such un-
guided, immoral and useless education."

II

Pushkin's love of freedom, both personal and
political, thus remained as strong as ever. But
his firmness in this respect did not exclude a
change of mind with regard to revolution, a
change which was due not to the Tsar's magnanimity but to his own study of history during
his seclusion at Mikhaylovskoye. While poring
over volumes of history,[1] he could not but medi-
tate upon the cementing and constructive forces
in a nation's growth. It was the continuity as
well as the stability of such forces that Pushkin
now wanted to see working in harmony with the
democratic liberal-progressive ideas so dear to
him. As a Russian nobleman he considered his
old nobility not so much a privilege as an obliga-
tion of a moral and at the same time æsthetic
order. Unwilling to confuse democracy with
plebeianism, that is, with the levelling-down
tendency, he rejected revolution in so far as it
often involves such a tendency. And he rejected

[1] At that time Pushkin read above all Karamzin's *History of the
Russian State*, but gradually he widened his historical knowledge
by reading the works of Guizot, Mignet, Thierry, Barante, etc.

it because he realised that levelling down could never lead to true freedom but only to anarchy, or else to tyrannies from below. It is interesting that some ten years later (in 1836) Pushkin, as though foreboding the dangerous and perhaps inevitable substitution of plebeianism for democracy in the modern world, wrote the following passage about the impressions of certain travellers in America: "It was with surprise that they saw democracy in all its disgusting cynicism, with its cruel prejudices, its intolerable tyranny. Everything noble and disinterested, everything that raises the human mind, is there squashed by inexorable egoism and by the passion for comfort."

Freedom used and abused for the sake of such purposes is bound to degenerate into its own parody. But are the masses ready for freedom? And if so, are they prepared to sacrifice everything to it, including their personal interests and appetites? Pushkin's contact with professional revolutionaries, during his stay at Kishinev and Odessa, had failed to provide the longed-for answer. Nor could he glean much hope from the abortive revolts in Naples and Spain. Despondent about it all, Pushkin wrote as early as 1823 in one of his letters: "Recently I was full of remorse, and while looking at Western Europe I turned to the Gospel; after which I wrote an imitation of the parable of that moderate democrat Jesus Christ." The parable

45

of that "moderate democrat" is about the
sower in the wilderness, and here is Pushkin's
version of it:

> Sower of Freedom in the waste,
> Before the morning star I rose;
> With fingers innocent and chaste
> I planted in a servile soil
> The seed from whence true being grows.
> In vain I trod laborious ways
> And squandered noble thought and toil . . .
> Graze on, ye peaceful peoples, graze!
> Ye'll never answer honour's urge.—
> Do herds need freedom? They were made
> For pole-axe, for the shearer's blade.
> From age to age their kind obeys
> The yoke that jingles, and the scourge.

Was it fair on the part of Pushkin to judge the
revolutionary efforts of his age by the meagre
results achieved under the blight of the Holy
Alliance, or by the "new Leonidases" of the rear
whom he had watched in the streets of Kishinev?
The truth is that he began to differentiate more
and more persistently between freedom and
revolution. Whereas his sceptical attitude towards the latter also came out in his great poem
André Chénier (1825), he never wavered in his cult
of freedom. An eloquent proof is his *Message to
Siberia*, which in 1827 he secretly sent to the
Decembrists through the wife of one of the con-
demned, who was on her way to rejoin her husband:

46

Entombed beneath Siberian soil
Be proudly patient in your pain:
Your soaring vision and your toil
　　Will not have been in vain.

The faithful sister of Distress,
Hope, in the pits that darkly yawn
Will waken joy and cheerfulness;
　　The longed-for day will dawn:

To you that in the darkness dwell
Friendship and love will find a way,
As to you in your convict cell
　　My free voice sounds today.

Then will the heavy fetters fall,
The prison crumble; freedom's words
Will greet you by the dungeon's wall,
　　Your brothers bear you swords.

Nicholas I was right in his distrust of Pushkin and of his political camouflage. Aware of the fact that the Tsar's hopes and admonitions had failed, the authorities did not stand on ceremony with the poet. Although nominally free, he could never get rid of the watchful eyes of the Third Section and of its chief, Count Benckendorff. And since Benckendorff was the intermediary between the Tsar and the poet it was he and his personal caprices that Pushkin had first to deal with in his contacts with Nicholas I. Nor did the Tsar's censorship exempt his works from that imposed upon all. What this double censorship was like can be seen from a letter in which he complained to Benckendorff: "Not a single Russian author is more oppressed than I. Having been approved by the Emperor, my writings are yet stopped when they appear; they are printed with the censors' wilful corrections, while all my protestations are ignored." Pushkin's position thus remained as difficult as ever. It became even more so after his marriage to Natalia Goncharova.

III

Pushkin met Natalia as a girl of sixteen in 1828, at a ball in Moscow. Struck by her beauty, he fell passionately in love. In the spring of 1829 he proposed, but the cautious Mme Goncharova gave a vague answer which was neither consent nor rejection. Yet however much entranced by Natalia's beauty, Pushkin must have had occasional doubts and misgivings: there were certain things likely to put him on his guard. As if anxious to distract himself, or perhaps to escape from the dilemma altogether, in 1829 he made a journey to the Caucasus and from there to the Turkish town of Erzerum, beleaguered at the time by the Russian troops. A proof of his uncertainty may be the love-poem he wrote in one of the most beautiful spots on the way to Georgia, thinking not of Natalia, but (if one is to judge by a few further unfinished lines) of some older love: perhaps of Maria Rayevskaya.

The hills of Georgia are veiled in misty night;
  Below, Aragva's waves are streaming.
I'm sad and yet serene; my very grief is bright,
  My grief that, born of thee, is dreaming
Of thee, of thee alone. . . . There's naught can
    make to pause
  My sorrow's pangs, disturb their quiet mov-
    ing. . . .
My heart takes fire again, and loves once more—
    because
  No way it knows to cease from loving.

Nor did he quieten down on his return. In
Moscow he was received coldly and rudely by
Mme Goncharova, who at the time was under the
impression that her daughter was being seriously
courted by Prince Meshchersky—in her opinion
much more eligible than Pushkin. She probably
did not mince her words either, since the poet
left for Petersburg in haste and more despondent
than ever. The wish to go abroad and escape
from it all beset him once more in January 1830,
when he wrote to Count Benckendorff: "As I am
neither married nor tied down to civil service, I
would like to undertake a journey to France or
Italy. If this is impossible, I beg you to grant
me a permit to visit China as a member of the
mission which is now leaving for that country."
Benckendorff's reply, ten days later, was as
fatherly as it could be: "In answer to your letter
of January 7th, I beg to inform you that His
Majesty the Emperor does not deign to grant your
request with regard to a journey abroad, since

49

such a step on your part would be a strain on your finances and would moreover take you away from your work. Further, your wish to accompany our mission to China cannot be granted in view of the fact that its personnel is already completed."

Meanwhile Prince Meshchersky must have disappointed the hopes secretly cherished by Mme Goncharova. Nor were there any signs that other suitors would come forward—Natalia being without a dowry. So in February 1830 one of Pushkin's Moscow friends suddenly brought to him the heartiest greetings of both Mme Goncharova and her daughter. Overjoyed, Pushkin hurried to Moscow, and on the Easter Sunday of 1830 his proposal was accepted. Mme Goncharova still refused to regard him as quite "respectable"; but since the Emperor himself seemed to take an interest in him, things might turn out all right after all, even if he was a poet. Another disturbing feature was that Natalia was not particularly in love with Pushkin, and he knew it. Fascinated by her beauty, he could no longer give her up, and only hoped to win her heart in time. "Habit and long intimacy will perhaps enable me to win the affection of your daughter," he wrote to his prospective mother-in-law. "In her consent to become my wife I see only the quiet indifference of her heart."

It is quite possible that Natalia attracted Pushkin as much by her coldness as by her beauty,

which was so devoid of flaws that one of his
friends defined it as "inanimate." Spoilt by his
numerous easy conquests, Pushkin was now confronted with something not so easy. But there
was a deeper and more serious side to it: his
determination to change his life and give it a
more stable basis. Not long before, on his
twenty-ninth birthday, he had written this gloomy
lyric, characteristic of his inner disquiet:

> Thou useless gift, that Chance did proffer,
>   Life, why wast thou granted me?
> Granted, why condemned to suffer
>   Through thy secret destiny?
>
> Whose summons, filled with hostile urging,
>   From the Nothing called me out,
> Shot my soul with passion's surging,
>   Mortified my mind with doubt?
>
> No goal awaits me for the morrow;
>   My heart is void, my thought is vain;
> And I am harrowed by the sorrow
>   Of life's unvarying refrain.

Pushkin's determination to marry was but a
proof that he had reached the most serious crossroads in his life. Tired of his former casual
amours, he longed for a more permanent affection
just as he longed for a greater equilibrium and
depth in his inner life. At the same time he
probably hoped that married life might give him
a certain social basis which would perhaps shield

51

him from all sorts of Benckendorffs, and bring with it independence. But however much he loved Natalia herself, there was little to be elated by in her impoverished and pretentious family. Mme Goncharova—a lewd and bigoted hypocrite whose husband had lost his reason—was a compendium of all the narrow-minded, philistine characteristics which he loathed. Apart from periodical quarrels with his prospective mother-in-law, there were also financial problems to be attended to before his marriage, and these were the more urgent because he knew that Natalia had no money. One can well imagine in what a mood Pushkin went, after one of such quarrels in the autumn of 1830, to the estate Boldino (on the Upper Volga), which his father had given him as a marriage settlement. His intention was to stay there only a short while in order to put things in order, but owing to a sudden outbreak of cholera in the district he was obliged to remain for several weeks, and these were the most remarkable weeks of his life.

As Pushkin himself recognised, he could always write best in the autumn. But that autumn he was full of inner problems and dilemmas which demanded a solution, and he could solve them only as a poet. So he wrote a prodigious number of masterpieces—lyrics, miniature plays, stories—in a comparatively short time, during which process he regained some of his serenity. He felt the strain of being separated from his betrothed.

Yet it is significant that in a minute of perfect frankness he said in a letter to his friend Pletnyov: "You have no idea how nice it is to run away from one's fiancée and to write verses. Oh my dear, what joy!" It was at Boldino too that he remembered, with unusual intensity, Amalia Riznich (who had died meanwhile in Italy), and wrote three poignant lyrics in which as it were he took his final leave of her. But neither his present nor his future seemed particularly bright:

My path is sombre; fraught with toil and sorrow
The storm-encompassed ocean of tomorrow.

Thus he complained in a poem (written at Boldino) without, however, submitting to his despondent moods. When on December 5th he returned to Moscow, new complications arose, and Pushkin had even to buy Natalia's trousseau. But always a realist, he now looked upon his married future rather soberly, as we can gather from his letter to N. I. Krivtsov on February 10th, 1831, i.e. only a few days before his marriage: "You are without a leg, and I—am married. Married—or almost so. I have examined everything that one could say in favour of a bachelor's existence. In cold blood I have weighed all the pros and cons of my new position. My youth has been spent noisily and without results. Until now, I have not even lived as people usually live. I have not known happiness. *Il n'est du bonheur que dans les voies communes.* I am over thirty. At thirty people marry as a rule, so I am doing what other people do, and I hope I shall not regret my step. Besides, I am entering marriage without intoxication, without childish enchantment. I see my future not as strewn with roses but in its austere nakedness. Sorrows will no longer surprise me; they are in my curriculum. What will surprise me is joy. But I am in a depressed mood to-day, so I will cut short my letter in order not to infect you with my worries: you have enough worries of your own."

IV

Pushkin's married life was not unhappy at first. He was sincerely in love with Natalia, but one of his acquaintances likened the newly-wedded couple to Venus and Vulcan. "I am married and happy," Pushkin wrote to Pletnyov. "My only wish is that nothing in my life should change: it could not be better than it is. This is such a novelty for me that I feel like one re-born." After a few weeks in Moscow the Pushkins left for Tsarskoye Selo and in the autumn of 1831 settled down in Petersburg, where Natalia's beauty was much admired. She made the best of it, and was quick to avail herself of the opportunities now opened to her. Social life was in full swing, but as its pleasures were by no means cheap they must have cost Pushkin much time and money. "I have no longer a bachelor's leisure, so vital for an author," he wrote to his extravagant Moscow friend, Nashchokin. "I am in a whirl of social engagements; my wife is in great demand; for all this I need money; money can be procured only by work, and in order to work I must have solitude." But solitude was out of the question. Penury and debts began to loom large on the horizon. To make things worse, Natalia was noticed by Nicholas I, who was something of a connoisseur of female beauty. The contact between the Tsar and the poet was thus renewed, and ominously so.

The Tsar's real attitude towards Natalia, who soon became a brilliant society star, is not easy to assess. Always ready to be jealous, Pushkin once complained to Nashchokin that Nicholas I flirted with her "like a regular sergeant," but he had implicit trust in Natalia's loyalty. The Tsar certainly took a keen interest in Pushkin's wife, and in order to enable her to attend the exclusive Court balls he made Pushkin (on January 1st, 1834) a "gentleman of the chamber": a rank suitable for a youth of eighteen, but somewhat grotesque in the case of a married man of thirty-five and a great poet into the bargain. It was an insult in the guise of an honour, and Pushkin felt it as such. "His Majesty expects me to speak to him of my new duties with gratitude and humility," he wrote in his diary. "I may be his subject, even his slave; but I shall never be a

flunkey or a buffoon—not even at the Court of
our Lord in Heaven."

One of Pushkin's unpleasant duties, from now
on, was to accompany his wife to the Court balls
and mix with the people who despised him and
whom he despised—people to whom genius meant
even less than to Natalia. Count V. A. Sollogub[1]
says in his *Memoirs* that the "poet of freedom, in
the company of his beautiful wife, and attired in
the Court uniform, played a part which was
pitiable, almost ridiculous. He was no longer
Pushkin, but only a courtier and a husband. This
he felt deeply. In addition, life in high society
made considerable demands upon his finances,
which were none too good. In order to make up
for it he began to gamble, but like all people in
need of money kept losing. Lastly, he also had
plenty of literary enemies who gave him no peace,
and wounded his pride."

It is quite possible that Pushkin was dragged
within the orbit of Court life not only as *le mari de
madame* but for more subtle reasons. The *débâcle*
of the Decembrists had made autocracy and
reaction triumph over the liberal-progressive ideas
formerly voiced by Pushkin. But those ideas now
began to stir up the budding intelligentsia. So
it was necessary to turn Pushkin into a Court
figure in order to compromise him in the eyes of
the liberal younger generation. And worst of all,
the trick succeeded, or at least promised to suc-

[1] A friend of Pushkin, once quite in vogue as an author.

ceed, at a time when Pushkin was doing all he could to extricate himself from the gilded morass of the "Court rabble." But it was no longer an easy matter to get rid of it. As children were added to his family his financial liabilities became so great that he was obliged to borrow from the Treasury, a step which only led to further complications of his already difficult position. He owed money to usurers, to friends, to acquaintances, and there was no prospect of any betterment.

Meanwhile, his wife's social successes were at their height. There were no proofs that she was unfaithful to her husband. On the other hand, her behaviour caused considerable gossip in society. Tired of it all, Pushkin wished to hand in his resignation and to leave Petersburg altogether, but was dissuaded on the ground that the Emperor might interpret such a step as an act of ingratitude. He stayed on with the secret hope of escaping to Mikhaylovskoye, where he would live a human life dedicated to creative work and to things which he regarded as real. Some time in 1836 he addressed to Natalia the following lines:

'Tis time, my friend, 'tis time. . . . The weary
    heart craves peace;
The swift days scurry past, and with each day
    decrease
Life's scanty particles, while, heedless, you and I
Think but to live. . . . And see, all turns to dust:
    we die.

57

Life holds no happiness save peace and liberty;
Long now a lovely dream has soothed my inner
    sight;
Long now, exhausted slave, have I designed to flee
To some far dwelling-place of toil and chaste
    delight.

But his wife thought differently. Now that she
was so popular at the Court and in society she
would not bury herself in the country, far from
her balls and admirers. The winter of 1835–6
was particularly trying for Pushkin, whose former
zest and love of life seemed to be on the wane.
Quite in the style of Leopardi's *fango è il mondo*,
he wrote to his friend Mme Osipova at Trigorskoye: "The world is a filthy lake of slime."
That slime now threatened to engulf him, and his
irritation grew from day to day. According to
one report (by I. I. Ivanitsky), Count Sollogub
had the impression that Pushkin suspected by
then a secret liaison between Natalia and the
Tsar, and was therefore determined to find death
in some way or other. Yet the same Sologub says
in his *Memoirs* that Pushkin was jealous of Natalia
not because he doubted her loyalty but from fear
of society gossip and ridicule.

Be this as it may, Natalia was being persistently
courted by d'Anthès, a handsome French refugee
with a commission in the Russian Guards.
Having been adopted by Baron Heckeren (the
Dutch Minister at Petersburg), d'Anthès became

a *habitué* of the best salons in the Russian capital, and was apparently determined to increase his social prestige by the conquest of Pushkin's wife, in which ambition he was being encouraged by the Baron himself. One of Pushkin's biographers, P. V. Annenkov, contends that Heckeren, who was sexually inverted and jealous of his adopted son, encouraged his advances to Natalia in the hope that a quarrel with Pushkin would ensue and separate for good the smart young gallant from Natalia. Pushkin's Moscow friend Nashchokin seemed to have been of the same opinion. Another surmise would have it that d'Anthès behaved as he did mainly in order to serve as a screen for the liaison between Natalia and the Tsar. There is no definite proof to support such a view. In May 1836 Pushkin wrote to Natalia from Moscow: "About you, my dear heart, there circulate some rumours which are only partly reaching me, because husbands are always the last in the town to learn about their wives' doings; still, it seems that your flirtation and cruelty have driven someone to such despair that, as a solace, he has now made for himself a regular harem out of the theatrical pupils. That's not the thing, my angel."

The fact that he could banter about this "someone," who was none other than the Tsar, proves that Pushkin still trusted his wife, although by that time he was probably concerned with her loyalty rather than with her love. The prospect of being ridiculed as a deceived husband was more than he could endure. He certainly must have felt cooler towards Natalia, with whom he had inwardly little in common—a state of things it did not take long for him to discover. As early as 1833 he had jotted down (in a draft) these words addressed to Countess Darya Fiquelmont, the charming Russian-born wife of the Austrian Ambassador: "I am created to love you and to follow you. Any other preoccupation on my part is either blundering about or sheer madness." Had Natalia been able to satisfy all his needs, hopes and longings, such a note to another woman could never have been written. And when Natalia's two sisters, Catherine and Alexandra, joined his household, he soon found he had much more in common with Alexandra, who was an enthusiastic admirer of his poetry, than with his own wife. While gossip and slander threatened to bespatter his name, he thus felt increasingly out of gear not only with society but also with himself. And since there was no escape from the "lake of slime" around him, his only reaction to it was a spiteful though helpless defiance. His state of mind can best be gauged by the following unfinished poem, in which he anticipated madness as the only outlet:

> Let me not laugh a madman's laugh!
> Better a beggar's scrip and staff;
>   Hunger, and toil, and care.—

Not that my mind I value so
Or would not freely let it go:
   That loss I'd gladly bear.

If they would only let me be,
To rage my madness, wild and free!
   Through woodlands dark I'd range;
Sing madly in a fiery haze;
Forget my being, in a maze
   Of dreams uncouth and strange.

I'd hear the waters whisper soft,
And, filled with gladness, gaze aloft
   Into the empty sky;
Freedom I'd know, and strength, and joy,
Like whirlwinds that the crops destroy
   And rend the woods awry.

But if by madness you're possessed
The whole world dreads you like the pest:
   They grant you no escape;
Bind you in chains to still their fear,
And at you through the grating peer,
   And tease you, like an ape.

And not the note of nightingales,
The whispering breeze in leafy vales
   I'll hear, when moonlight wanes;
But my poor comrades' crazy call,
The warders' oaths behind the wall,
   And shrieks, and clanking chains.

V

So much for the once gay and carefree Pushkin.
Anonymous letters of the usual kind made their

appearance before long. In one of them he was obligingly informed (in French) that the "Most Serene Order of the Cuckolds had elected M. Alexander Pushkin to be the Deputy Grand Master and Historiographer of the Order." In the "diploma" which conferred upon him such a high honour there was a nasty hint that the Tsar himself was one of those responsible for the poet's marital misfortunes.

Suspecting d'Anthès and Baron Heckeren of being the authors of the letter (copies of which had been sent also to his friends), Pushkin challenged d'Anthès to a duel. Both "father" and "son" were in a state of alarm. It is quite possible that Heckeren had written that letter, or had had it written, in order to shift Pushkin's rage from d'Anthès to the Tsar. At the same time he was fully aware that a duel with Pushkin would impair his own diplomatic career. So he was anxious to avert the duel—even at the cost of persuading his "son" to marry Natalia's sister Catherine. In the end the gallant Frenchman avoided the duel by proposing to Catherine, whom he actually married and jokingly referred to as *ma légitime*. Pushkin refused to have anything to do with this unexpected brother-in-law. But it soon transpired that d'Anthès' marriage was only a pretext for further advances to Natalia. On discovering that he had cunningly enticed Natalia to a secret meeting with him at the house of one of her women friends, Pushkin reacted in such a way that a duel became inevitable. It took place on January 27th, 1837. Pushkin was mortally wounded and died two days later, at the age of thirty-eight.

His death caused a great sensation, and the house wherein he lay in state was besieged by crowds of mourners: intellectuals, students, artisans. All classes were represented among those who paid homage to the dead poet; all except the "cream" of society, now concerned about the fate of their darling d'Anthès. The Minister of Saxony at St. Petersburg reported to his government that at least 50,000 people must have come to express their grief.

Nicholas and his police became alarmed when the poet's death took on the character of a national calamity. Quick action was imperative in order to avoid incidents at Pushkin's funeral, and Count Benckendorff took the necessary measures. After a secret funeral service in the Royal Stables Church, Pushkin's body was removed by the Tsar's police at night. The coffin, covered with a mat and straw, was driven, under the escort of gendarmes, in an ordinary sledge all the way to the Svyatogorsky monastery near Mikhaylovskoye, where the poet was buried.

It should be said in fairness that Nicholas I treated Pushkin's family generously. Ample provision was made for Natalia and the children. The Tsar also settled the poet's debts, which were by no means small. A few years later Natalia

63

married General Lanskoy and, as far as one knows, "lived happily ever after."

Heckeren and his "son" had to leave Russia, but without detriment to their subsequent careers. The Baron eventually became a highly respected *doyen* of the diplomatic corps in Vienna, while d'Anthès flourished as a financier and politician and was raised to the rank of Senator in Paris. Both of them lived to what is usually called a venerable old age.

Chapter Four

Pushkin as a Phenomenon

I

IN spite of her eagerness to make up for lost opportunities in the past, Russia, between Peter the Great and Alexander I, failed to express herself adequately in terms of literature. What the world now understands and admires under the name of Russian literature came with and after Pushkin. Yet Pushkin is perhaps the only world-classic whose work is either unknown or else taken only on credit outside his own country. The principal reason is of course the fact that Pushkin is one of the most difficult authors to translate. And he is difficult mainly on account of his apparent obviousness and simplicity. It has almost become a custom to refer to him as the Mozart of European poetry. Trite though this comparison may be, it still holds good. Pushkin's lucidity and dancing ease are "Mozartian" in the best sense of the word. No matter how deep and painful his inner experiences, he usually expresses them in the simplest manner imaginable. It does not take long, however, to discover that this simplicity is complexity crystallised and transmuted—by a kind of verbal alchemy—into poetic forms, the very perfection of which gives the impression of spontaneity. While giving much joy to a reader, it is more than likely to be a translator's despair.

Equally astonishing is the wealth of literary *genres* in verse and in prose which Pushkin handled with such skill as to raise the level of Russian literature to a height which became a standard for subsequent generations. According to the famous critic V. Belinsky (1811–48), "all previous Russian poets compare with Pushkin as rivers, big and small, compare with the sea. His verse started a new era in the history of Russian poetry. And what verse it is! Antique plastic power and classical simplicity blend harmoniously in it with the enchanting melodies of the romantic rhyme. The acoustic wealth and all the might of the Russian tongue find here an astonishingly complete expression." Pushkin knew how to turn, by a secret of his own, even ordinary conversational language into great poetry. He despised the use of "purple patches," of rhetorical and ornamental trappings. Combining *mots justes* with his flair for the poetic value of each individual word, for the right cadences, sounds and alliterations, he wielded in everything he wrote a sense of measure and harmony which is all the more surprising if one remembers that temperamentally he was inclined to excesses—a feature probably due to his somewhat fantastic racial origin. Whereas on his father's side he belonged to the old Russian nobility, his maternal great-grand-father, Hannibal, was an Abyssinian princeling—bought by the Russian ambassador on the slave-market in Constantinople and sent as a present to Peter the Great, who took care of his education and his subsequent career.

Pushkin's intense and passionate personality was often suggestive of hotter climes than that of Russia, and some of his acquaintances were rather puzzled by his impulsive character. His one-time friend, the great Polish poet Adam Mickie-wicz, even thought him "much too impressionable and at times irresponsible." Yet (as Cherny-shevsky put it) he was endowed with that higher "moral health which imparted upon all his attachments and inclinations a refreshing luxuriance and vitality." He was inwardly too rich and too intensely alive to achieve perfect self-mastery as a man. But he certainly achieved it as a poet. The one was thus sublimated and fulfilled by the other. However impulsive or "irresponsible" he may have been in ordinary everyday life, in his literary work he showed such discipline and balance that he is often referred to, and without exaggeration, as a Hellene of the North.

II

There is only one poet in European literature who equals Pushkin in this respect: Goethe. But Goethe's harmony was largely a result of

67

deliberate and almost methodical self-discipline, accompanied by that serious "will to culture" which in Germany has always been so much stronger than culture itself. In addition to being a poet, Goethe was also a thinker, a scientist and a man of action, whereas Pushkin's thoughts and ideas were a spontaneous by-product of his artistic genius rather than a result of his deliberate will or effort. Far from identifying the man with the poet, Pushkin drew a line between the two. In one of his poems he frankly confessed that in the ordinary circumstances of life he was perhaps weaker than the least significant of mortals; but no sooner had he been summoned by the call of his own genius than he fled from the "idols of the day" to regions accessible only at rare moments. This was not an escape from himself or from life, but only a condition in which he could achieve a maximum of creative intensity and concentration. And as for his "irresponsible" lightheartedness, it was often only a mask, hiding his profound inner seriousness in things that really matter. He was perfectly familiar with tragic moods and even with moments of nihilistic doubt which threatened to damp down all his youthful "thrill of freedom, glory, love," as we can gather from this description of his own Mephistophelean demon and tempter:

> Bitter as wormwood were our meetings;
> His smile, the way his eyes would dart

With malice, his sarcastic greetings
Poured chilly poison in my heart.

An endless stream of defamation
On Providence his tongue would drip;
He called the beauty of creation
A dream, at ardour curled his lip.

In freedom nor in love believing,
At life with scornful callousness
He cavilled, in all nature leaving
Nothing that he could wish to bless.

Add to this his insatiable thirst for life, which
was only another expression of his vitality seeking
for an outlet, and you will understand his
"broadness." The gamut of his experiences
was in fact so wide that one is not surprised if
some of them remained in a more or less raw,
unsublimated state even when turned into
technically perfect verse. But caprices of this
kind could by no means prevent him from
reaching such heights as are recorded in his
Prophet (1826)—a poem in which Pushkin intertwined Goethe's dictum *stirb und werde* (die and
become) with the profoundest notion of his own
calling. The poem is worth quoting as one of the
rare instances in which Pushkin availed himself
of the solemn biblical tone, without sacrificing
to it his dynamic restraint.

With spiritual thirst aflame
Weary through empty wastes I wandered;

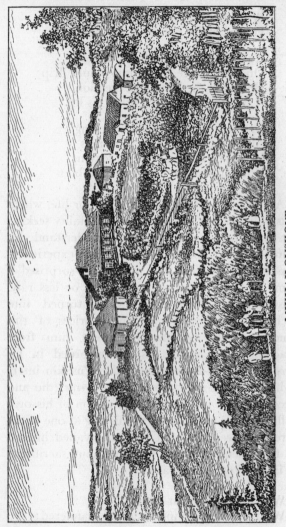

MIKHAILOVSKOYE.

And lo, a six-winged seraph came
To meet me where the paths were sundered.
With touch as soft as sleep he laid
His fingers on my lids, and made
My eyes to open, wide and wise,
Like to a startled eagle's eyes.
He laid his fingers on my ears,
And they were filled with noise and ringing:
I heard the trembling of the spheres,
The angels through the heavens winging,
The beasts that creep beneath the tide,
The vine that climbs the valley-side.
And to my mouth he closely clung
And wrenched away my sinful tongue
That dripped with vanity and cunning;
He pressed my fainting lips apart
And in them thrust a serpent's dart,
Red blood about his fingers running.
With his sharp blade he split my breast
And thence my trembling heart he stole,
And in its stead a burning coal
Into the gaping wound he pressed.
Long in the desert dead I lay,
Until at last I heard God say:
"Rise, prophet, filled with My commands;
Become all sight, become all hearing,
And journey over seas and lands,
Men's hearts with fiery utterance searing."

It would be impossible to imagine a greater
distance than that between the frivolous *Gabriliada* and *The Prophet*. But in the space between
these two extremes there moved Pushkin the man,
avid for all kinds of experiences, which he absorbed
and then distilled into poetry. However painful

71

some of these may have been, his process of creation usually enabled him to sublimate them and thus rise above them. It was in this manner that his serene affirmative attitude towards life triumphed over his darkest moments of gloom and despondence. Hence he could be deeply tragic, but hardly ever pessimistic. His *Yes* to life proved always stronger than his despair—an attitude which is perhaps best expressed in the well-known elegy he wrote in the autumn of 1830, only a few weeks before his marriage:

The frenzied merriment of misspent years
Like wakening from wine my spirit sears;
Like wine, the poignant imprints of past pain
Grow stronger in me, as in years they gain.
My path is sombre; fraught with toil and sorrow
The storm-encompassed ocean of tomorrow.

And yet, my friends, I do not ask for death;
Life I desire, for pain and contemplation;
Again I shall be stirred by pleasure's breath
Mid all my sorrow, care and agitation;
Again at times with music I shall throb,
My fancy's fruits again will make me sob;
And maybe, as my last sad days decline,
Love with a farewell smile on me will shine.

A poem such as this can put a new complexion on Pushkin's light-heartedness and insouciance. What he really aimed at was not a light-hearted but a full life, which he did not want to encumber by any preconceived "philosophies," attitudes or dogmas. His intuition of life came from life itself in all its diversity. This explains the mark of authenticity, so typical of everything he wrote. It is here that we come upon Pushkin's *essential* realism on the one hand and his wide range of interests on the other. The two were in fact interdependent. And when this range was transferred upon the plane of culture and history, it was enough to turn Pushkin into one of the broadest and most universal poets in European literature.

III

Pushkin's universality in this respect was so great as to disregard any limits of space or time. As a poet he felt at home in any country and in any age. One of his critics aptly remarked that Pushkin "could think and speak as a pagan, a Christian, a medieval knight, a Renaissance man, a votary of Voltaire and a disciple of Rousseau." But in spite of this he was far from being a cosmopolitan eclectic; he remained thoroughly himself both as a creative personality and as a Russian. While professing to be a "good European" (and living up to it), Pushkin was yet deeply rooted in his native soil and tradition. Unwilling to separate the destinies of Russia from those of Western Europe, he was convinced that the two were complementary rather than antagonistic, and therefore necessary to each other. When in 1836 P. Chaadayev, in his notorious *Philosophic Letter*, belittled Russia's achievements as compared with those of Western Europe, Pushkin was quick to send him an answer in which he disagreed with his friend, pointing among other things to this fact: "The division of the Churches separated us from Europe. This is beyond doubt, and so we did not participate in many of those great events which agitated Europe. But we too had a mission of our own. Russia, such as she was, swallowed up all the Mongolian victories at her own cost. The Tartars did not dare cross our western frontier and leave us in their rear. They retreated into the steppes, and Christian civilisation was thus saved."

It was Pushkin's sense of life's values that nourished his intuitive understanding of the processes of life in their historical and cultural manifestations. This explains his broad universal interests and sympathies which, as a Russian, he extended to everything his country was able to absorb creatively. One of his critics in the middle of the last century (Apollon Grigoryev) said that "the sphere of Pushkin's inner sympathies excluded nothing that was before him, nothing that will be truly and organically ours after him." Following him along this path we come, however, once again to the idea of a synthesis between Russia and Europe—this time on a purely cultural ground. Nothing illustrates such a notion better than the bulk of Pushkin's work, in which the

finest artistic traditions of the West are perfectly
blended with the true spirit of Russia. It was
perhaps for this reason that Gogol saw in Pushkin
a representative of the Russian man "as he may
become, in the course of his development, two
hundred years hence." It was for the same reason
that Dostoevsky, too, some forty years later,
insisted in his *Diary of an Author*, as well as in his
Pushkin speech in 1880, that the greatest Russian
poet contained enough substance to feed and to
direct the literature or even the culture of the
whole of nineteenth-century Russia.

What Dostoevsky appreciated in Pushkin was
above all the fusion of the Russian spirit with his
characteristic all-embracing universality. But the
latter was regarded by him as an essentially
Russian feature as well. Hence his paradoxical
conclusion that Pushkin was the most national of
Russian poets precisely because he was so
universal: "Emphatically I say that there has
never been a poet like Pushkin, a poet with his
universal sympathy, his extraordinary depth,
and the miraculous reincarnation of his spirit in
the spirit of other nations—miraculous, because
this gift has never been repeated in any other poet
in the world. This universality is to be found
only in Pushkin. And so I repeat that he is a
phenomenon, a prophetic phenomenon, because
in his poetry he expressed the national spirit of
our future which, already, has come to pass.
For there is no power in the spirit of the Russian

nation if it be not the power to aspire to universality and to an all-embracing humanism."

We need not be disturbed by Dostoevsky's superlatives. He meant what he said; and what he meant was that Pushkin's work as a whole embodied the nearest approach to that cultural synthesis between Europe and Russia which Dostoevsky himself saw as one of the tasks to be aimed at and perhaps achieved by Russia. In this respect, at any rate, Pushkin was a "prophetic phenomenon." And since among those Western elements which helped to shape his work and his genius English literature played a most important part, he is among other things a vital cultural link between Great Britain and Russia. This fact alone is enough to enhance the interest of English readers in Pushkin.

Chapter Five

Pushkin's Poetry

I

IN discussing Pushkin one is struck by the difficulty of finding a definition which would cover all his works. A classicist, a romantic and a realist in turns, he defies any attempts at being reduced to a single literary school or to any specified "ism." Yet his supremacy in Russian poetry, from Lomonosov onwards, remains unchallenged. Lomonosov had introduced into Russian prosody the regular tonic metre (prevalent also in German) as being the most suitable poetic medium in so far as his native tongue was concerned. Pushkin brought that medium to the height of flexibility and perfection. Parallel with that there was a less conspicuous trend modelled on the rhythm of the folk-song or even more frequently of the pseudo-folk-song, which created a tradition of its own and reached its climax in the work of Alexander Koltsov (1808–42) and Nikolay Nekrasov (1821–77). This trend, too, found in Pushkin one of its exponents, although in the bulk of his poetry he adhered to Lomonosov's principle. He even adopted the simple four-footed iambic, advocated by Lomonosov, as his favourite metre. But whatever metre he used, he entirely abolished the declamatory eighteenth-century manner and imparted to his poems a new inflection, a new texture, and above all a conversational ease, combined with a short-hand realism the dynamic condensation of which carries one far beyond mere visual effects even in his descriptive verse. Take the beginning of his poem *The Avalanche*, in which he records one of his Caucasian impressions:

> Beaten by jagged rocks to steam,
> Before me pours the boiling stream;
> Above my head the eagles scream,
>   The pine-wood speaks,
> And through the mist there faintly gleam
>   The mountain-peaks.

Only six brief rhythmic lines, and the picture is complete—not in its repose, but in its sweeping flux or movement which evokes corresponding emotions in the reader. With what simple touches he can produce a maximum of effect and at the same time stir up the desired mood is shown by the opening verse of his long and magnificent *October 19th, 1825*, in which he commemorates the annual foundation day of the Lycée:

> The autumn wood casts off its crimson gown,
> The faded field is silvered o'er with frost,
> The sun peers forth, a sad, reluctant ghost,
> And hurriedly behind the hill goes down.

Burn brightly, pine-logs, in my lonely cell;
And thou, O wine-cup, that in autumn rains
Dost comfort so, in my sad heart instil
A brief oblivion of bitter pains.

Equally amazing is the evocative concreteness
of everyday things which he turns into poetry.
Take his *Winter Evening*, or such an obvious picture as we find in these few lines of *Evgeny Onegin*:

Winter! the peasant's heart now dances;
Again he journeys on his sleigh.
The old mare sniffs the snow, advances
With shambling trot, as best she may.
The little cart is bravely swinging,
The powdery snow from ruts upflinging;
In sheepskin coat and belt of red
The driver perches at its head.
Next in his little sledge's traces,
Pretending to be horse—and there
Black puppy sits, as passenger—
With freezing hands, the houseboy races;
The rascal smarts, and grins the more
For mother, threatening at the door.

Here, if anywhere, the most ordinary trifles,
expressed in everyday language, have become
great art. One could quote a number of equally
simple examples of that visual, rhythmic and
musical unity which was one of the secrets of
Pushkin's verbal instrumentation. This applies
to his lyrical and epic verse alike. And no matter
how profound the inner experience thus expressed, his art never ran away with him. He

79

remained its master, knowing how to impart the character and the *verve* of spontaneity even to those poems which had cost him a great deal of labour. However agitated his private life, his work always preserved that lucid "sanity of genius" which is perhaps inalienable from artistic integrity. Unable to be turgid and stilted, he could not be false in whatever he wrote. The truth of art meant to him not a distortion of the truth of life, nor a refuge from it, but a sublimation of it in terms of beauty. Hence his dread of everything grandiloquent and "cleverly" hollow —a dread which made him prefer even "silly" simplicity to all sorts of rhetorics. "Your verses are too clever," he wrote in May 1826 to his friend Vyazemsky. "Poetry—may the Lord forgive me!—ought to be a bit silly." Which was an intelligent definition of his own attitude towards poetic creation.

II

When Pushkin began to write, the eighteenth-century classicism with its severe division of *genres* was already disintegrating.[1] So he was destined to play a double rôle as a poet: while completing the eighteenth-century currents, he at the same time led the way to modern Russian literature.

[1] This process was partly due to the influence of Thomson, Gray, Young and Ossian, whose poetry was being translated and discussed towards the end of the eighteenth and the beginning of the nineteenth century.

Having paid due tribute to the conventional poetry of the previous age, as well as to the intimately personal verses of the romantics (who deliberately confused the various *genres* and insisted on originality at the expense of convention), he eventually superseded both schools. He even had a brief spell of Ossianism, and this at a time when Voltaire and Parny were among his chief influences. From the French, he learned above all technical neatness, lucidity and that gay if often malicious wit which found a corresponding echo in his own nature. It was not for nothing that, while still a boy, he wrote his first verses in French, a language he knew so well that his nickname in the Lycée was "Frenchy." Pushkin took a particular liking to Voltaire. He read *La Pucelle* at the age of fourteen, and was so impressed by it that under its influence he embarked upon a similar immature epic of his own, *The Monk* (1813), the first three cantos of which have been preserved. As for his Russian predecessors, he appreciated what was truly excellent in the poetry of the "Tartar" genius Derzhavin. Technically, he learned a good deal from Zhukovsky, even if he remained a stranger to his sentimental romanticism of the "beyond." What attracted him much more was the earthy and pagan Batyushkov whose *My Penates* was responsible for one of Pushkin's best-known early poems, *The Little Town*, written during his Lycée period.

The curriculum of the Lycée encouraged the pupils' interest in Russian literature. There was a certain rivalry in writing poetry among Pushkin's school-fellows, two of whom—Delvig and Kyukhelbeker—subsequently became famous. It was in the Lycée also that Pushkin's poetic genius bore its first fruits in the style typical of the period: light, fugitive, witty and polished. The neat anacreontic eighteenth-century trend (mixed with pastoral motives and with a kind of Staffordchina eroticism) prevails, as we can see from the poem *Reason and Love*, written in the Lycée as early as 1814.

Daphnis, pursuing Doris through the grove,
"Stay, fair one, stay!" he panted; "do but say
'I love you,' and I'll never bar your way
Again—I swear it by the God of Love."
   Reason advised: "Say not a word!"
   Said Eros: "Say, 'My heart you've stirred!' "

And Doris said, "You strangely stir my breast,"
And their two hearts succumbed to love's sweet
   spell;
Then at her feet, adoring, Daphnis fell,
And her shy gaze his lowered head caressed.
   Reason admonished: "Run away!"
   And naughty Eros whispered: "Stay!"

She stayed, and he his trembling fingers laid
Upon her hand, and her he closer drew,
And "Look," he whispered, "how they bill and
   coo,

82

That pair of doves, beneath the lime-tree's shade."
   Reason repeated: "Run away!"
   Said Eros: "Study how they play!"

Over the maiden's burning lips there passed—
A moment there, then gone—a fleeting smile;
Then on her eyes a mist descended, while
Into the shepherd's arms she sank at last.
"Be happy!" Eros whispered in her ear—
And Reason said no word that she could hear.

Conspicuous at that early age are his sprightly
conversational epistles, epigrams, descriptive,
satirical and (now and then) frivolous verses,
constructed in such a manner as to stress the witty
pointe at the end—again quite in the style of the
eighteenth century. Obviously, he was still an
apprentice, but an apprentice of genius, waiting
for his chance. This was offered to him when, on
finishing the Lycée in 1817, he settled down in
Petersburg. In spite of the hectic life he led there
with his boon companions, he yet found enough
time for poetry, in which he now became more
flexible and more mature. He was particularly
good at elegies, epigrams and such rebellious
poems of indictment as the already quoted *In the
Country* and *The Dagger*.

Belonging to that progressive portion of the
gentry which foreboded the crisis of a transition
from the feudal agricultural to a bourgeois-
capitalistic system of life, Pushkin could not but
sympathise with the most liberal ideas of the

period, or for that matter with the prospective Decembrists. On the other hand, his creative freedom was even dearer to him than any political activity, in which he never felt quite at home. The principal work written by him during his Petersburg period (1817–20), *Ruslan and Ludmila*, has in fact nothing to do with politics. It is a playful tale in six cantos, told for its own sake. Externally a mild skit on romanticism, it is yet romantic in Pushkin's sense; and in his sense romanticism was "Parnassian atheism," i.e. a rejection of hide-bound literary *clichés* and dogmas in the name of one's own creative independence. He certainly struck here a new path in Russian poetry. Everything in this poem was new to Pushkin's contemporaries: the verse, the wit, and even the fairy-tale element with its ingeniously interwoven echoes of Voltaire, Ariosto, Wieland's *Oberon* and of the Russian chap-books. There is a hint in it of the folk-sagas or *byliny*, notably those of the Kiev cycle with Prince Vladimir and his heroes in the centre, but the spirit of the poem is still that of an eighteenth-century romance, or of the ballets so fashionable in those days.

The opening of *Ruslan and Ludmila* takes us to Prince Vladimir's Court at the moment when he is celebrating the marriage of his daughter Ludmila to the valiant champion Ruslan. But after the wedding-feast Ludmila is suddenly snatched away by the dwarf and magician, Chernomor, who takes her to his far-away palace.

84

Ruslan and three of his less successful rivals set out, each on his own, in the hope of rescuing the princess. The poem consists of their adventures during that quest. After a series of reverses Ruslan penetrates into Chernomor's hiding-place, where he recovers his bride, captures the long-bearded dwarf and returns triumphantly to Kiev.

The fanciful pattern of the poem, its humour and ease marked a break with the pompous solemnity of the classical epics. The more so because the inflection of the poem remained throughout that of the spoken word. Some of Pushkin's expressions were so "ungenteel" that they aroused much anger among the traditionalists. Its sparkling buffoonery on the other hand, its eroticism and frankly epicurean attitude towards life, were a tonic after the somewhat unctuous quietism of Zhukovsky, whose sentimentally romantic poem *The Twelve Sleeping Maidens* Pushkin parodied in one of the cantos. Both the tone and the language of *Ruslan and Ludmila*, representing a successful application of Karamzin's "middle style" to poetry, opened up two further possibilities: the *conte* in verse (in the tradition of La Fontaine, or of Byron's *Beppo*) and that homely type of the "novel in verse" which Pushkin gave later in his *Evgeny Onegin*. In spite of the polemics it provoked, *Ruslan and Ludmila* became something of a milestone and inaugurated the most brilliant period, a veritable Golden Age, in Russian poetry. In addition it was a step forward in the process of democratising poetry, without lowering its highest standards. It certainly provided a link between literature and the people, even if its folk-quality, its "Russianness," was still purely decorative and external.[1] Zhukovsky, having read *Ruslan and Ludmila*, presented its author with a portrait inscribed, "to the victorious pupil from his defeated teacher." No higher tribute could have been paid, at the time, to a poet just out of his teens.

III

Ruslan and Ludmila established the fame of Pushkin, who was by then an exile in Southern Russia. This "Southern" period was responsible for his Byronic interlude, so important for his development as a poet. A complementary influence was that of the French poet, André Chénier, whose short, wonderfully balanced "anthological" manner appealed to Pushkin even during his romantic period. The fact should be stressed that Russian romanticism as a whole had neither the broadness nor the *élan* comparable with the romantic movement in some other European countries. Its fierce opponent, the critic N. I. Nadezhdin, refused to see in it anything except the aping of foreign literary fashions.

[1] Pushkin made up for this by the magnificent (and utterly untranslatable) *Prologue*, summing up the spirit of Russian folklore, which he added to the second edition of *Ruslan and Ludmila* in 1828.

For one thing, in Russia the romantic movement was not so deeply conditioned by life with all its social, political and mental crises as was the case in the West. And secondly, severe censorship made even a romantic protest against the official strait-jacket imposed upon life a dangerous venture, unless it was camouflaged by that "Æsop's language" in which some of the subsequent Russian authors became great experts. The only outlet was indirect criticism of the age, i.e. criticism from the standpoint of the self-centred, dissatisfied or frustrated ego, and in this respect Byron proved a strong incentive.

Scope for the romantic *mal du siècle* and its concomitant—the romantic protest—was provided in Russia by the atmosphere of Alexander's last years and the "leaden regime" of Nicholas I. Little wonder that Byron, the poet of freedom, found some of his most ardent admirers among the Decembrists. But quite apart from the secret societies, the formation of which was itself a protest, a poet with Pushkin's love of independence and freedom was bound to raise his voice in a country where the Childe Harold type was not mere abstraction but reflected the warped individual as a reality of the period. It was Pushkin who first naturalised in Russia this "superfluous" Byronic or Rousseauesque-Byronic character, with his futile nostalgia for something better and more genuine, that is, more natural, than the system of life in which he felt a stranger. *The*

Prisoner in the Caucasus (1820–21, published 1822) was the first "Byronic" tale in verse, in which Pushkin confronted a contemporary individual with an unspoilt child of nature mainly in order to show the incompatibility of the two. The action takes place in the Caucasian mountains where a kidnapped Russian—a cultured society youth, belonging to a world totally different from that of his captors—is the central figure. A half-savage Circassian girl falls in love with him, but the sophisticated man of culture acquits himself badly in this new situation. He seems to be so devastated by scepticism, disillusions, and also by the frustration of his previous love, that he is no longer capable of any profound or spontaneous emotion. Tired and devoid of all fire of life, he fails to respond to the girl's generous love even when she frees him from his shackles and thus enables him to escape. He callously swims to safety over the same river in which she commits suicide because of her unrequited passion.

It can hardly be said that this egotist, who is nearer to Chateaubriand's René than to Byron's vigorous adventurers, is as concrete as are the majority of figures created by Pushkin. He is a shadow rather than a three-dimensional character, but this itself may have been due to Pushkin's intention "to depict in him that indifference to life and to its pleasures, that premature mental old age which is so salient a feature in the youths of the nineteenth century," as he confessed in a letter to his former schoolfellow V. P. Gorchakov. Besides, the centre of gravity of this romantic poem lies more in the realistic background (as distinct from Byron's fanciful East) than in the love-drama. Pushkin's pictures of the mountaineers' manners and ways of life are surprisingly concrete. Nor does he sentimentalise their primitiveness, but shows them as they are: reckless, hardy and cruel.

A masterpiece of descriptive and dramatic realism is Pushkin's second Byronic tale, *The Robber Brothers* (1821–2, published in 1825). Having started his exile in Ekaterinoslav, Pushkin saw in 1820 how two convicts, chained to each other, jumped into the Dnieper, swam to its eastern bank and escaped. Always keenly interested in the folk-songs and tales about the Volga brigands, especially those about the legendary seventeenth-century dare-devil Stenka Razin, he modified the theme accordingly. Surrounded by a throng of outlaws and desperadoes, Pushkin's robber describes how he and his brother, although chained together, escaped by eluding their prison guards, and how in consequence his younger brother died, tormented by fearful visions during his delirium. This powerful poem is supposedly a fragment of a work planned on a bigger scale, but never completed or even resumed.

Different in theme and in treatment is *The Fountain of Bakhchisaray* (1822), a romantic "Eastern tale" with a Crimean background, and written

in mellow, languorous verse, perfectly adjusted to
the subject-matter.[1] The love drama described in
it had apparently happened in the harem of the
Crimean Khan Ghirey,[2] and its story is both
simple and exotic. Having brought from one of
his expeditions the beautiful Polish Princess Maria
Potocka as his captive, Khan Ghirey neglects his
former favourite, Zarema. And as the Christian
girl-captive will not hear of love, Ghirey's passion
is fanned into obsession. Driven to despair by
jealousy, Zarema kills her rival, and is herself
cruelly put to death by her master. Pushkin
brought this theme of unrequited love from his
stay with the Rayevsky family in the Crimea,
where he had visited the fountain at the Khan's
decayed residence in Bakhchisaray. Maria is
supposed to be a portrait of the Maria Rayevskaya
who had repudiated Pushkin's own love—perhaps
the sincerest love he had ever experienced, and
the memory of which meant so much to him.

IV

If *The Fountain of Bakhchisaray* is the most
Byronic of Pushkin's tales in verse, his *Gipsies*
(1824, published 1827) already marks his tendency to free himself from Byron and romanticism. It is a very dramatic tale and at the same

[1] Published in 1824, this poem aroused violent polemics
between the classicists and the romantics.

[2] Pushkin's Ghirey is slightly suggestive of Hassan in *The
Giaour*, while the jealous Zarema makes one think of Gulnare in
The Corsair.

time so condensed that Prosper Mérimée, who translated it into French and published it together with his own *Carmen* (1847), said: *Pas un mot à retrancher, et cependant tout est simple, naturel.*[1] This time the setting was provided by the Bessarabian plains where the memory of another exiled poet, Ovid, still seemed to linger and was suitably recorded by Pushkin. Aleko, the hero of *The Gipsies*, is a further development of *The Prisoner in the Caucasus*. He too is a self-centred Byronic-Rousseauesque seeker for freedom. Disgusted with society and civilisation, he joins a band of Bessarabian gipsies, roams about as one of them, loves and is loved by the gipsy *belle* Zemphira, who is unable to fathom why her lover had given up everything in order to become a homeless gipsy.

ZEMPHIRA: Tell me, my friend, do you not regret
All that you left behind for ever?
ALEKO: What have I left?
ZEMPHIRA: You know quite well:
Your countrymen, your cities.
ALEKO: Why should I regret? If only you knew,
Or could imagine
The curse of stuffy cities!
There the people, herded behind their walls,
Know neither the freshness of the morning
Nor the spring fragrance of the meadows.
They fear to love, they banish thought,
They barter with their own freedom,
They bow their heads before their idols
And beg for money and for chains.

[1] "Not a single word could be taken out, and yet the whole of it is simple and natural."

What have I left? The bitterness of treachery,
Calumny and prejudice,
The unreasoned persecution of the mob,
Or else gilded shame.[1]

As in *The Prisoner in the Caucasus*, Pushkin confronts a civilised *déraciné* with a primitive community, but carries the dilemma and also the test of the hero much farther. Zemphira, whom Aleko loves, is a child of nature. Free as a bird, she trusts the spontaneity of her emotions as they come and go, and does not acknowledge any compulsory ties or obligations. Once her passion for Aleko is spent, she falls in love with another gipsy as spontaneously as she had previously chosen Aleko, and is brutally frank about it. Aleko's own love of freedom now undergoes a trial which is too much for him. Unable to grant Zemphira the liberty that is hers by nature, he murders in a fit of jealousy both her and her young lover. The gipsies, with Zemphira's aged father at their head, do not exact a blood vengeance. Horrified at the crime, they only expel Aleko as a misfit, himself a victim of the vices of the society from which he had fled.

> Leave us, proud man!
> We are wild, we have no laws,
> Yet do not torture, do not kill,
> We have no use for blood or groans;
> But with a murderer will not live.

[1] This is a very inadequate literal translation. In the original the poem is in rhymes.

Seeking freedom for yourself alone,
You were not made for our savage ways;
Your very voice fills us with horror:
For we are gentle, kind at heart,
While you are of a reckless, evil mind
         —leave us, then,
Farewell, and peace be with you.

The Gipsies thus unmasks the Byronic hero by revealing his inner blind-alley. Whatever Aleko may stand for, he personifies the bankruptcy of romantic self-centredness ("seeking freedom for yourself alone") and even more the inability of a civilised man to run away from civilisation, "back to nature" or, for that matter, "back" to anything. Such a flight or regression is always forced and therefore insincere, unreal. Pushkin, who was at the height of the civilisation of his time, knew something about this, and said it as powerfully as he could. But parallel with this *leitmotif* the poem includes the drama of jealousy to which Pushkin was not a stranger either; his Odessa love, Amalia Riznich, had seen to that. *The Gipsies* may even have some bearing upon one of his own adventures in the same Bessarabian plain which serves as a background for the poem. According to an account heard from a witness and printed in the Russian periodical *The Years Gone By* (1908) by a certain Z. K. Railli-Arboret (an active revolutionary in the 'seventies), Pushkin himself was in love with a gipsy-girl and lived for a while with the gipsies near a place called

Yurcheni. "The camp was headed by an aged *buli-basha* (elder) much respected by the gipsies. The old man had a beautiful daughter called Zemphira. She was tall, had big black eyes and long plaits. Zemphira walked about dressed like a man, in bright trousers, sheepskin cap and embroidered Moldavian shirt, and smoked a pipe. The rich necklace of gold and silver coins adorning that wild *belle* must have included gifts from many an admirer. Pushkin was so struck with her beauty that he stopped for several days at Yurcheni. He actually settled down in her father's tent. Zemphira and he roamed about for days, and but for Zemphira's sympathy for a young gipsy the idyll would have continued. It was jealousy that brought it to a sudden end. One morning Pushkin awoke in the *buli-basha's* tent to find that he was alone. Zemphira had disappeared; she had run away to Vazareshti. Pushkin hurried there, but when he arrived she was already gone, having undoubtedly been warned by the gipsies. Later it transpired that Zemphira had been murdered by the enamoured gipsy."

V

Pushkin took from Byron the new pattern of poetic narrative with its fragmentary character, its lyrical tonality and its romantic themes. But having done this he went his own way, dictated to him by that interest in external reality which gradually led him to *Onegin* and later to prose. With the completion of *The Gipsies* he shed his own Byronic period, but not entirely. Some of its elements, duly modified, lingered on in his work. Nor did he discard the structural pattern of the Byronic tale in verse, but perfected it instead. In his excellent but unfinished *Tazit* (often called *Galub*, 1829-33) he returned to Caucasian themes and characters, obviously as a result of his journey in 1829. This time the romantic *leitmotif* was a pretext for developing a clash between the primitive moral values on the one hand and those inculcated by a higher, i.e. Christian, code on the other.[1] There are Byronic touches also in his chief work, *Evgeny Onegin*, but this need not disturb us. Pushkin made use of Byron only as a stepping-stone towards his own originality and his essentially Russian consciousness. Neither Byron's rhetoric nor Byron's pose could ever infect him, since they were not in his character. To quote Belinsky again, "Byron attracted him not as an ideal to be followed, but as a phenomenon, as a champion of the ideas of his age, and Pushkin paid tribute to each important phenomenon of the age. Yes! Pushkin was an expression of the world in which he lived; but that was also a Russian world and Russian humanity."

[1] The theme also implies, as it were, the moral superiority of the Russians who were engaged in conquering or in pacifying the Caucasus.

Having absorbed all the Byronic elements he needed, Pushkin was not in the least afraid of further influences in so far as he could turn them to his own use. Among these, Shakespeare became particularly prominent for a while. His sprightly *conte* in verse, *Count Nulin* (1825, published in 1827), unites the influences of both Byron and Shakespeare, while yet remaining thoroughly Pushkinian. It is a subtle parody of *The Rape of Lucrece* (in a realistic Russian setting), told with the humorous verve reminiscent of *Beppo*. Pushkin gives the following account of its genesis. "Towards the end of 1825 I was re-reading in my village Shakespeare's rather weak poem *Lucrece*, and thought to myself: What would have happened had Lucrece come upon the idea of giving Tarquin a smack instead? His enterprising spirit might perhaps have cooled down and made him retreat with shame. Lucrece would have been saved from suicide, Publicola from his fury, and the world and its history would have taken a different turn. The idea of writing a parody of Shakespeare's story tempted me so strongly that I could not resist it, and in two mornings the tale was finished."

The gist of the tale can be told in a few words. During his journey from Paris back to Petersburg, Count Nulin's carriage breaks down and he stays overnight in the nearest manor, where the pretty hostess's husband happens to be away. At night the Count suddenly decides to play the part of

Tarquin and steals into his hostess's bedroom. But once there he is administered such a slap by the lady of the house that he beats a shameful retreat in the name of morality triumphant. In the morning the hostess meets her would-be Tarquin at the breakfast-table as though nothing had happened. He is introduced to her husband, just back from the hunt, and then politely departs. Finally, the fellow who laughs with satisfaction at the virtuous exploit of this up-to-date Lucrece is not her husband but a young and handsome neighbour, who happens to be her lover. All is told with economy and with that incomparable humorous inflection which was one of Pushkin's most enviable gifts.

VI

His chief title to glory is however his lyrical poetry, in which he reached the height of perfection between 1824 and 1831, that is, between his banishment to Mikhaylovskoye and his marriage. The two years of compulsory loneliness on his mother's estate enabled him to enlarge his knowledge of literature and also to deepen his own inner life. It was at Mikhaylovskoye that *The Prophet* was written. So were *October 19th, 1825*, *Winter Evening* and a number of other lyrics in all of which the form and the contents are equally indivisible. One seems to have grown out of the other so organically that it would be as difficult to alter his verses as to reshape a crystal. His favourite metre was the iambic, but he could put into the regularity of any metre an astonishing variety of rhythm and music. While Pushkin the man provided the starting-point, Pushkin the poet transmuted the raw material of life into something which imbued his personal impressions and experiences with a wider universal significance. His poem under the bald title *Verses Written during a Sleepless Night* (1830) can serve as an illustration. However personal the moment it records, it is yet hauntingly pertinent to everyone who reads it.

> Sleep evades me, there's no light.
> Darkness wraps the earth with slumber,
> Only weary tickings number
> The slow hours of the night.
> Parca, chattering woman-fashion,
> Night that offers no compassion,
> Life that stirs like rustling mice—
> Why encage me in your vice?
> Why the whispering persistence
> Of a day departed twice?
> What black failures do you reckon?
> Do you prophesy or beckon?
> I would know whence you are sprung,
> I would study your dark tongue.

Another example of such a transmutation of personal "raw material" of life is his *Memory* (1828), one of the finest poems he ever wrote.

When trade and traffic and all the noise of town
Is dimmed, and on the streets and squares
The filmy curtain of the night sinks down
With sleep, the recompense of cares,
To me the darkness brings nor sleep nor rest.
A pageant of the torturing hours
Drags its slow course, and writhing in my breast,
A fanged snake my heart devours.
My fears take form, and on the wearied brain
Grief comes in waves that overflow,
And Memory turns a scroll to tell again
A legend that too well I know.
Reading the past with horror, shame and dread,
I tremble and I curse,
But the repentant tears, the bitter tears I shed,
Will not wash out a single verse.

It is true that much of Pushkin's lyrical
poetry reflects, either openly or by implication, the various phases of his own inner life.
But it is equally true that they can be read
and enjoyed by themselves apart from any
personal associations with the poet, although
these may contribute to a better understanding
of such poems as *Arion, October 19th, 1825* or
"Let me not laugh a madman's laugh." His love-
lyrics on the other hand, even the most intimate among them, are so clear that they
always explain themselves, no matter whether
we have any personal data or not. Three of
his love poems may be quoted to this effect,
the first containing an old and yet eternally new
theme :

I loved you. Even now I may confess
Some embers of my love their fire retain.
But do not let it bring you more distress—
I do not want to sadden you again.
Hopeless and tongue-tied, yet I loved you dearly,
With pangs the jealous and the timid know.
So tenderly I loved you, so sincerely,
I pray God grant another love you so.

The simplicity of this little poem (1829)
renders to perfection the complicated emotional
state of love half-spent and vacillating, accompanied by a premonition of parting, by the
reminiscence of the once intense feeling, as well
as by a sad yet generous resignation to one's loss—
all in eight lines. And the more intensely personal the experience recorded, the more universal
becomes its appeal once it has been conveyed to
us through Pushkin's concrete and plastic verse.
One of his most personal poems, the sonnet
Madonna (1830), recalls how his "African"
sensuality was transmuted—under the sway of
his fiancée's beauty—into a feeling of well-nigh
religious reverence and adoration. Yet in spite of
such an autobiographical touch, the sonnet can
be read as a detached little masterpiece of general
significance.

My dwelling to embellish, ne'er did I
Want many paintings, by old masters done,
That simple visitors should gape, and run
To hear the experts' learned How and Why.

In that still nook where I slow labours ply
One picture I desired to see; but one:
Where from the canvas, as from out the sky,
The Holy Virgin and Her blessed Son,

Alone in Zion, with no angel choir,
Should mildly gaze—She in majestic tire,
He wisdom-eyed—and in bright glory shine.

My wishes have been heard. The Lord has sent
Thee down to earth, to me, Madonna mine,
Of purest beauty purest bodiment.[1]

The personal element prevails, however, in the
following poem (1830), which can be mentioned
as a complement to the sonnet. For while
describing the change of his own turbulent
passion into something nobler, it seems to contain
also a veiled hint at his "Madonna's" emotional
coldness.

No, never think, my dear, that in my heart I
    treasure
The tumult of the blood, the frenzied gusts of
    pleasure,
The groans of hers, those shrieks: a young Bac-
    chante's cries,
When writhing like a snake in my embrace she
    lies,
And wounding kiss and touch, urgent and hot,
    engender
The final shudderings that consummate surrender.

[1] In July 1830 he wrote in a letter to his betrothed: "I comfort
myself by spending hour after hour in front of a painting of a
Madonna resembling you as one drop of water resembles
another."

How sweeter far are you, my meek, my quiet
    one—
By what tormenting bliss is my whole soul undone
When, after I have long and eagerly been plead-
    ing,
With bashful graciousness to my deep need
    conceding,
You give yourself to me, but shyly, turned away,
To all my ardours cold, scarce heeding what I say,
Responding, growing warm, oh, in how slow a
    fashion,
To share, unwilling, yet to share my passion.

The same glowing intensity permeates the
poems inspired by Mme Riznitch and the love-
lyric he addressed to the beautiful Mme A. P.
Kern (1825), whom he met (after an interval of
six years) at Mme Osipova's in Trigorskoye. As
this is one of his best-known poems it deserves to
be quoted in its entirety.

I can remember our first meeting,
When like a miracle you came
Before my eyes a swiftly fleeting
Vision of beauty's purest flame.

Amid the miseries that oppressed me
Amid the world's vain foolish cries
For long your gentle voice caressed me
Your features gleamed before my eyes.

The years went by, wild storms swept past me
Scattering many a youthful dream;

I lost the voice that once caressed me,
I lost your features' heavenly gleam.

Shut in my prison's dark damnation,
Before me stretched dumb days, dead years,
Deprived of God, of inspiration,
Deprived of love, of life, of tears.

Then from its trance arose in greeting
My soul as once again you came
Before my eyes a swiftly fleeting
Vision of beauty's purest flame.

My heart is beating with elation
As from the dead once more arise
Glory of God and inspiration,
Life, love and tears to fill my eyes.

It is not without interest that in a private letter
Pushkin referred, later on, to the same Mme Kern
as a "Babylonian whore"—a characteristic he must
surely have been aware of at the time he addressed her in the poem as a "vision of beauty's
purest flame." But beauty, in his eyes, redeemed
and transformed everything within its sway. What
for Pushkin the man may have been a "Babylonian whore," became the opposite for Pushkin
the poet. He was thus capable, during the
process of creation, of turning a theme into
something which had nothing in common with
the starting-point itself. His *Legend* about the
medieval quixotic knight who had devoted his
life to the worship of the Madonna is a proof.

From the recently examined drafts it is clear that Pushkin first chose the theme in a frivolous or even cynical mood, and intended to treat it as a joke. But during the process of writing all the dross fell off, and finally the poem became an apotheosis of the eternal feminine as understood by a medieval worshipper of the Holy Virgin. Pushkin himself was neither a philosopher in a narrow sense nor a religious seeker, but he had a profound sense of values which usually came to his rescue. Nor was he unfamiliar with the torments of spiritual thirst: his *Prophet* vies with Isaiah both in contents and in its clarion-like call to man's highest self-realisation. Another of his poems, *The Pilgrim*, was inspired by Bunyan's *Pilgrim's Progress*. There are quite a few religious motives in the verses he wrote after 1831, although as a man he showed hardly any interest in religion. His preoccupation with the more alarming irrational themes (as long as he could express them in terms of art) came out in a number of his poems, and he was capable of singing the praise of life even in the teeth of the elemental calamities hostile to man:

> War knows the dizziness of drink,
> Like the abyss's gloomy brink,
> The darkness of the storm-tossed ocean,
> The fatal heaving of her breast,
> Arabian sands in wind-swept motion,
> The fetid breathing of the pest.
> And all that brings the threat of death

For hearts that beat with mortal breath
The secret holds of wordless pleasure;
The pledge, perhaps, of deathlessness!
Happy the mortal who this treasure
Amid life's violence makes his!

The negative and merely destructive aspects of such "wordless pleasure" can be felt in one of Pushkin's finest poems, *The Egyptian Nights* (1835), where the decadent Cleopatra offers herself to chance lovers in order to gloat afterwards over their death as the price of her caresses. Another flash from the same dark depths of human nature comes out in his *Anchar* or *The Poison-Tree* (1828), a poem the ominous character of which is conveyed by its very rhythm. The theme may have been suggested by Coleridge's *Remorse*, as well as by Byron's references to the upas-tree in *Childe Harold*; yet Pushkin worked it out independently into a gruesome and incredibly compact symbol of evil:

The sun-tortured, thirst-racked steppeland
Gave it birth in a day of wrath,
And fed the dull green of its leafage
And its roots with a poisoned broth.

No bird ever lights in its branches,
No tiger approaches the tree;
Alone, the black storm-winds brush it
And, venom-infected, flee.

This agent of death and destruction is avoided by every living creature, but not by man. Driven

by his lust for power, a ruler sends a slave to the
Poison-Tree with secret orders which are promptly
obeyed.   On his return, the slave

> brings with him poisonous resin
> And a branch with a few faded leaves,
> And the sweat on his pallid forehead
> In thick streams trickles and cleaves.
>
> The poison he brings, and fainting
> At the feet of his dread lord lies
> On the bast that the tent-floor covers.
> He utters no word, and dies.
>
> But the king, in that poison steeping
> His arrows with secret art,
> To his enemies sends destruction
> And death on each poisoned dart.

A thorough account of Pushkin's lyrics and
other short poems would require a study of a
different size.   Suffice it to say that Dostoevsky's
epithet "universal" can fully be applied to him
in this respect too.   The number of his themes
and motives, not counting his fugitive occasional
verse, is staggering.   And he handled them as one
of the unsurpassed masters of the word in
European literature.

VII

As for the tales in verse written by Pushkin
after his Byronic period, *Poltava* (1828) and *The
Bronze Horseman* (1833) should be dealt with before
106

we proceed to his central work, *Evgeny Onegin*.
In the interval between the two, he wrote at
Boldino in 1830 his humorously realistic *Little
House in Kolomna*, the introductory octaves of
which read like a witty exposition of his own *art
poétique*. Kolomna is a suburb of Petersburg, and
so the characters presented are lower-middle-
class people: a widow, her daughter and the
daughter's lover, who settles down in their little
house disguised as a female cook until, one
morning, he is found by the girl's mother in the
process of shaving. Written in octaves, this tale
is a distant echo of Byron's *Beppo*, and stands by
itself amongst Pushkin's creations. It differs
from his other tales in verse, and especially from
Poltava and *The Bronze Horseman*, which with all
their dissimilarity have one thing in common:
the poet's interest in Peter the Great. Deeply
concerned with the historical destinies of his own
country, Pushkin was so fascinated by that
revolutionary on the throne that for a time he
intended to write a history of his rule, but finally
erected a lasting monument to him in these two
poems instead.

Poltava is dedicated to an anonymous woman
who is most probably Maria Rayevskaya, and it
comprises two themes. One of them is Maria
Kochubey's tragic love for the Ukrainian *hetman*
(an equivalent of viceroy) Mazepa, the hero of
Byron's tale from which Pushkin took the epigraph.
But whereas Byron described one of Mazepa's

youthful adventures in a romantic halo, Pushkin portrayed him at the height of his career and true to history: as a cruel, vainglorious old intriguer plotting with the Swedish king Charles XII against Peter the Great. The first two parts of the poem are concerned with the theme Maria-Mazepa. Maria, a proud and stately beauty who was in love with the aged *hetman*, ran away from her parents in order to be with him. Eventually her own father was executed by the *hetman*'s order and, crushed with grief, Maria lost her reason. Such was Mazepa's revenge on his one-time friend Kochubey who, resentful because of Maria, had denounced the *hetman*'s plot to the Tsar, while the Tsar, refusing to believe it, denounced Kochubey himself to Mazepa. But here the second theme comes in: the contest between Peter I and Charles XII for supremacy in the north of Europe. With Mazepa's help and connivance the Swedish king penetrated into the heart of the Ukraine where, in 1709, he was defeated by Peter near Poltava—a victory out of which Russia emerged as a great European Power. The third part of the poem, which deals with this decisive clash between the two monarchs, ends with the flight of Charles and Mazepa. But this flight is only an anticlimax to the battle, at the height of which,

> like the voice of Heaven, urging
> The victors, Peter's voice sounds clear:
> 'Now with God's help, to work!' And here,
> His favourites about him surging,

Comes Peter from the tent. His eyes
Dart fire, his face commands surrender,
His steps are swift. The tempest's splendour
Alone with Peter's splendour vies.
He goes. They bring his charger, panting,
High-strung, yet ready to obey,
He scents the fire of the fray
And quivers. The blazing heat bores deeper.
The battle rests—a tired reaper.
The Cossack steeds, paraded, shine.
The regiments fall into line.
No martial music is redounding,
And from the hills the hungry roar
Of the calmed cannons breaks no more.
And lo! across the plain resounding,
A deep 'Hurrah!' roars from afar:
The regiments have seen the Tsar.

Poltava is thus divided between personal fates
and passions (Mazepa-Maria) on the one hand
and the problem of the historical destiny of
Russia (Peter-Charles XII) on the other. "Strong
characters, and the profoundly tragic shadow
hovering over all the horrors—this was what
appealed to me," Pushkin said in a letter. "I
wrote *Poltava* in a few days; but for that, I would
have given it up." The strong characters, Peter
and Mazepa, stand out also as the two contrasts.
While Mazepa's passions and ambitions are those
of a great egoist, Peter represents the idea of the
State, which is also his principal passion. In
spite of a certain lack of unity between its two
themes, this poem yet marks one of the summits

of Pushkin's creative power. Impersonal, terse, and metallic in its diction, it is the nearest approach to what might have been worked out into a great national epic, had Pushkin not been in such a hurry to finish it in "a few days."

' In contrast with *Poltava*, *The Bronze Horseman* is all of a piece. It is preceded by a magnificent eulogy of Peter and of Petersburg, which he had built on the Neva in the teeth of all the obstacles erected by Nature. But if Peter's will thus proved victorious, Nature took her vengeance in the shape of the Neva's periodic floods, which threatened to destroy what had been built by man. The worst flood within human memory was the one in 1824, and the havoc wrought by it in Petersburg (with Falconet's famous bronze statue of Peter the Great surging out of the waves) served as the background for the tragedy depicted in the poem. Originally, Pushkin intended to write a narrative in verse under the title *Ezersky*, which was to be also the name of the principal character—a humble *déclassé*, impoverished and gone to seed.[1] Among the literary influences that may have affected Pushkin in this case were two poems by his Polish friend Adam Mickiewicz: one of them, *The Monument of Peter the Great*, prophesied the symbolic downfall of the statue, while the other— *Oleszkiewicz*—gave a picture of the eve of the flood in 1824. Pushkin made the flood the starting-

[1] The advent of a bourgeois-capitalist era threatened many a gentry-family (including the Pushkins) with the same fate.

point of his poem, and the triumph (not the downfall) of Peter's monument its climax. The poem thus became a realistic-symbolic masterpiece the like of which had never before appeared in Russian. An idea of its excellence can perhaps be conveyed by this description of the flood:

                    Neva, leaping
Seaward against the blast
Was beaten in the strife at last,
Against the frantic tempest sweeping;
The people swarmed and crowded, curious,
And revelled in the towering spray
That spattered where the waves were furious.
But the wind driving from the bay
Dammed Neva back, and she receding
Came up, in wrath and riot speeding;
And soon the island flooded lay.
Madder the weather grew, and ever
Higher upswelled the roaring river
And bubbled like a kettle, and whirled,
And like a maddened beast was hurled
Swift in the city. All things routed
Fled from its path, and about it
A sudden space was cleared; the flow
Dashed in the cellars down below;
Canals above their borders spouted.
Behold Petropol floating lie
Like Triton in the deep, waist-high!
A siege! The wicked waves attacking
Climb thief-like through the windows; backing,
The boats stern-foremost smite the glass,
Trays with their soaking wrappage pass.
And timbers, roofs, and huts all shattered,
The wares of thrifty traders scattered,

And the pale beggar's chattels small,
Bridges swept beneath the squall,
Coffins from sodden graveyards—all
Swim in the streets!

In the midst of all the chaos there rises out of
the waves, in the Senate Square, the giant statue
of Peter the Great as calm and unperturbed as
ever. Seated on a rearing horse, the monarch
resembles a demon defying the wrath of Nature.
Opposite Peter's statue the "little man" (renamed
Evgeny) clings to a carved lion guarding the
terrace of the Senate building. It is not his own
safety he is worried about, but that of his sweetheart Parasha, whose hut in the outskirts of the
city is exposed to all the fury of the waves. When,
after the flood, Evgeny found that Parasha had
actually perished, he went mad. Week after week
he kept wandering about the streets, a beggar and
an outcast. But one cloudy night he suddenly
came once again to the Senate Square dominated
by the statue of the giant Horseman

Who, motionless, aloft and dim,
Our city by the sea had founded,
Whose will was Fate. Appalling there
He sat begirt with mist and air.

In a moment something flashed through
Evgeny's deranged mind. Vaguely aware of his
own misery, he suddenly realised that the cause
of it all was the Horseman who, for some reason

112

of his own, had built the accursed city on the
banks of the Neva. The poor wretch gazed at
the statue; then, threateningly and full of
indignation, he

> clenched his teeth
> And clasped his hands, as though some devil
> Possessed him, some dark power of evil,
> And shuddered, whispering angrily,
> 'Ay, architect, with thy creation
> Of marvels. . . . Ah, beware of me!'
> And then in wild precipitation
> He fled. . . .

For at his threatening gesture, the Horseman
stirred with so terrible a mien that the demented
Evgeny had to flee. And while

> rushing through the empty square,
> He hears behind him as it were
> Thunders that rattle in a chorus,
> A gallop ponderous, sonorous
> That shakes the pavement. . . .

Pursued by the ghostly horseman, Evgeny
escaped and dragged on his existence until, one
day, he was found dead from exhaustion in the
wreckage of the hut where he and Parasha had
formerly dreamed of happiness. The symbolic
meaning of the poem is clear. Less clear, however, is the answer to the question, how far the
giants of history are justified in sacrificing the
happiness of thousands of little men to a great
achievement. Goethe tried to give an answer in

the second half of his *Faust* (the fate of Philemon and Baucis). Even more radical was Nietzsche's answer in *Thus Spake Zarathustra*. Pushkin, on the other hand, was artist enough to abstain from answering. He only stated the problem, and he stated it with such poetic force that *The Bronze Horseman* is still considered the greatest poem in Russian literature.

VIII

The impersonal objectivity which, after 1831, was one of Pushkin's chief characteristics was responsible for another fascinating branch of his poetry: the *Skazki* or *Fairy-Tales* in verse. The beginning of the 'thirties was generally marked by an interest in folklore. The enormous success of Gogol's *Evenings on a Farm near Dikanka* (1831-2), so full of folklorist flavour, was a proof. A year later, Dahl's *Russian Fairy Tales* appeared. Peter Kireyevsky, Gilferding and scores of others took up Russian folklore in a scientific manner, and the results were rich indeed. Among the lasting monuments of their labours are the splendid collections of the *byliny* on the one hand and of A. N. Afanasyev's *Russian Folk-Tales* on the other. It all began with the problem of the "national" character of literature, to which Pushkin himself could not remain indifferent. But this problem too, or rather its connection with folklore, he solved in a manner of his own.

It will be recalled that twice before—in *Ruslan and Ludmila*, and then during his stay at Mikhaylovskoye—Pushkin showed a lively interest in Russian folklore; an interest which his nurse Arina must have stirred up in him while he was still a boy. Its purely external, decorative character in *Ruslan and Ludmila* has already been mentioned.[1] But while at Mikhaylovskoye he not only listened again, as in childhood, to Arina's tales but was anxious to deepen his contact with the simple folk by collecting their stories and especially their songs, which he and one of his friends, S. A. Sobolevsky, intended to publish. Some of his finest ballads, such as *The Bridegroom* (1825, written in the metre of Bürger's *Leonora*) and *The Drowned Man* (1828), abound in folk-flavour. So does his inimitable *Hussar* (1833), which can best be described as a humorous colour-print—the Russians call it a *lubok*—for the peasants, but transposed into poetry. The *Prologue* he wrote in 1828 (its first draft dates from 1824, that is, from Mikhaylovskoye) for the second edition of *Ruslan and Ludmila* is a poetic summing-up of the whole of Russian folklore; and its magical first lines about the wise cat walking upon a golden chain around an oak tree are an almost literal repetition of the introduction to a fairy-tale he had heard from Arina. Another example of how near to the language and the

---

[1] The same can be said of his earliest attempts of this kind in the poem, *Bova* (1814) where he tried to imitate the manner and the tone of folk poetry.

inflection of the people Pushkin could really come is his unfinished poem about the she-bear that was killed by a peasant. A proper rendering of its charm is impossible, since no European language can match the wealth of diminutives, the rhythmical peculiarities and what might be called "facial expressions" of Russian words. Still, these few opening lines may give some idea of its flavour in the original:

When in the warm springtime
Out of the little white daybreak,
Out of the forest, the dense forest
Came the dark Mrs. Bear
With her small bear-cub children
To walk a little, to look a little, to show their faces,
Mrs. Bear sat down under a birch-tree;
The bear-cubs began to play together,
To embrace, to wrestle,
To wrestle, to turn somersaults.

Pushkin returned to folklore in the 'thirties, and on a bigger scale. Here, once again, his "universality" came out in a quite peculiar manner. He not only wanted to bridge the gap between literature and the people, but made an attempt at adapting the themes taken from non-Russian folklore in such a way as to make them an organic part of both Russian literature and the Russian people. This explains his keen interest in the folk-poetry of some other nations as well. As early as 1828 he made a paraphrase of *The Twa Corbies*, and his Russian version is even more laconic than the Scottish original. Some time between 1831 and 1833 he adapted eleven poems from *La Guzla* (Prosper Mérimée's fake of "Illyrian" ballads) with such skill as to imbue them with the flavour of genuine folk-songs. Two Serbian folk-songs he translated from the originals collected and edited by Vuk Karadjitch. He also admired C. Fauriel's French version of Greek folk-songs, some of which had been rendered into Russian by the translator of the *Iliad*, the poet N. I. Gnedich. Nearest to his heart was, however, Russian folklore, in the spirit of which he wrote, between 1831 and 1834, his *Skazki* or *Fairy-Tales* in verse.

The title of the finest of them suggests a chap-book for the people: *The Tale of Tsar Saltan, of his Famous and Puissant Champion Gvidon Saltanovich, and of the Lovely Swan-Princess.* It is a tale of two sisters anxious to ruin their younger sister, whom Tsar Saltan had married; but through all sorts of strange happenings their machinations fail, and the ending is a happy one. The other *skazki*, stylised with equal success, are: *The Tale of the Dead Princess and the Seven Champions; The Tale of the Fisherman and the Fish; The Golden Cockerel; The Tale of the Parson and his Workman Balda.* Only one of these tales—the one about the parson and his workman (stylised like doggerel for the people) —was due entirely, and *The Tale of Tsar Saltan* partly, to the stories which Pushkin heard from Arina at Mikhaylovskoye in 1824. *The Tale of the Dead Princess* was based on the Grimm brothers' *Snow White* (*Schneewittchen*). So was *The Tale of the Fisherman*. The source of *The Golden Cockerel*, on the other hand, was the legend of the Arab astrologer in Washington Irving's *The Alhambra* (London, 1832), a French translation of which was found, together with the one of Grimm's stories (*Vieux contes*, 1830), in Pushkin's library.

Attempts at adapting motifs from borrowed fairy-tales to the Russian tone and spirit had been made, before Pushkin, by Zhukovsky. But in contrast to Zhukovsky's purely conventional Russian garb, Pushkin succeeded in bringing his own *skazki* so close to the people's style and flavour that his *Tale of the Fisherman*, for example, became a genuine Russian folk-tale and was later registered by Afanasyev as such. It matters little whether Pushkin took his themes from the Brothers Grimm or from Irving. The important thing is that he knew how to turn them into masterpieces which the Russian people could regard as their own and even include in the treasury of their lore. Here, if anywhere, Pushkin took the literary language out of Karamzin's drawing-room and imbued it with a new vitality coming from the people, thereby enlarging the scope of his literary achievements. But if we want to see Pushkin's genius in all its broadness and maturity we must go to his principal work—*Evgeny Onegin*.

Chapter Six

Evgeny Onegin

I

THE realistic and at the same time lyrical "novel in verse," *Evgeny Onegin*, occupies a central position in Pushkin's work as a whole. And since he wrote it over a number of years, its progress went hand-in-hand with the poet's inner growth, which it reflects. It can even throw considerable light on those of his lyrics which may at first have had some bearing upon the "novel." According to M. L. Gofman, the poetical thoughts and emotions indicated in *Evgeny Onegin* "gave rise to new poems in which the hints made in the 'novel' were fully worked out. And *vice versa*, Pushkin's lyrical poems contributed considerably to that basic tone which is typical of the plot of the novel, of its development, and which makes its portraits and characters live. The connection between Pushkin's lyrical poetry and this novel is so significant and so organic that the premature conclusion of the novel coincided with a certain lowering of his output in lyrical poems. It was not by mere chance that the years of his energetic and successful work upon this novel were also the years of his greatest lyrics."

Pushkin started the first chapter of *Evgeny Onegin* in May 1823, while still in Kishinev, and finished it in October. The second chapter was written in Odessa towards the end of the same year. The third chapter was begun in Odessa in February 1824 but was completed at Mikhaylovskoye in August. By the end of 1826 the fourth, the fifth and the sixth chapters were finished. The seventh chapter was written between March 1827 and November 1828. The original eighth chapter, depicting Onegin's journey, was begun at Moscow in September 1829, but completed only a year later at Boldino, where the original ninth—subsequently eighth—chapter was also written. As for the tenth chapter, most of it was burned (at Boldino in 1830) on account of its dangerous political hints and implications. The "novel" was brought into its present shape in 1831. In March 1833 the first complete edition appeared, and four years later the second.

Evgeny Onegin is written in that four-footed iambic which Lomonosov had already regarded as the most suitable metre for Russian poetry. Pushkin also chose it—partly because it brings poetry nearest to the inflection of conversational language. The "chapters" are divided into stanzas, and each stanza contains fourteen lines, the last two being a kind of *coda*. The pattern of the sonnet thus becomes evident, and quite a number of the stanzas could be spaced out accordingly. The metre is regular throughout, but this regularity does not interfere with the wealth of the rhythm, in which the poet achieves here some of his greatest triumphs.

Judging by the opening chapter Pushkin first thought of writing a more or less satirical work —something in the manner of Byron's *Don Juan*, as he himself acknowledged in a letter to Vyazemsky in November 1823. The work still retains a few touches of *Don Juan*: in the first place its realism and its frequent personal digressions, humorous, satirical or meditative. This is particularly true of the chapter which opens with Onegin's flippant monologue about his uncle, to whose death-bed he hurries as prospective heir, anticipating a tedious encounter.

"When Uncle in good earnest sickened
(His principles were always high),
My own respect for him was quickened;
'This was his happiest thought,' said I.
He was a pattern edifying,
Yet, heavens! how boring, and how trying,
To tend a patient night and day
And never move a step away!
And—then—how low the craft and gross is!—
I must amuse a man half-dead,
Arrange the pillows for his head,
And bring, with a long face, the doses
And sigh, and wonder inwardly,
'When will the devil come for thee?' "

Yet in the same chapter the intended satire gave way to a tolerant humour full of delightful realism. As the narrative continued, its realistic pictures of life were being increasingly permeated by lyrical moods and "atmosphere." What might, perhaps, have turned into a Russian counterpart of Byron's *Don Juan* thus became a lyrical "novel in verse." [1] The difference between the two has been admirably summed up by Mr. Desmond MacCarthy in his Foreword to the English edition of *Evgeny Onegin* (translated by Oliver Elton), and we could do no better than repeat his words on the subject. "*Evgeny Onegin* has been compared with *Don Juan*," he says, "yet a 'novel in verse' would hardly describe Byron's poem. With the exception of a witty passage or two, it is precisely in 'character-drawing' that *Don Juan* is weak. The strength of *Don Juan* lies elsewhere—in the careless vigour and brilliant vehemence of its commentary on life, society and politics; in its exhilarating changes of mood, back and forth from young desire to cynical burlesque, and from personal indignation to a pleased contempt of all the world. It is a hold-all into which a willy-nilly blurter of indiscriminate truths and falsehoods, about himself and anyone else, crammed whatever he burned to say at any moment. *Evgeny Onegin* has its digressions, too, but those are adjusted to the whole; while *Don Juan* is one long, loose, rich, unending flow of

[1] A satirical Russian equivalent of Byron's *Don Juan* would, anyway, have been impossible on account of the censorship. This may perhaps have been one of the reasons why Pushkin gave up his original intention.

splendid talk. The two poems have, however, one thing in common; both poets put into them their experiences in the social world. Pushkin's reckless life in Petersburg contributed to *Evgeny Onegin*; Byron's recollections in exile of London and Newstead Abbey come into *Don Juan*."

The entire first chapter, which introduces the hero, is mainly a description of Onegin's childhood and youth in the atmosphere of the smart Petersburg society. He was a somewhat stereotyped product of his class at a time when its prestige and prosperity stood rather high. So the routine of his life had to be stereotyped too, and was in fact laid out for him while he was still an infant. The same round of governesses and tutors, of conventions, of society accomplishments and of final boredom.

By Fate Evgeny was befriended:
First by a *Madame* he was tended;
Next came a *Monsieur*. But the child,
Though nice, was gay and rather wild;
And therefore, not to overwork him,
Monsieur l'Abbé, a needy Gaul,
With pleasant jesting, taught him all,
Nor would with moral strictures irk him,
But to the Summer Garden took
The tricky lad, with mild rebuke.

But when Evgeny was attaining
The age of youth and turbulence,
The age of hope and soft complaining,
They packed the Monsieur off; and hence

Onegin was no more imprisoned,
But like a London *dandy* dizened,
And cropped most fashionably, too;
And so at last the world he knew.
He could express himself completely
In French, and write it, and could prance
So light in the mazurka-dance;
Could bow so easily and neatly.
Enough; the world decides at once
He is a dear, and not a dunce.

II

When first introduced to us, Onegin is neither
a rebel nor a victim of the genuine *mal du siècle*.
Being a man of fashion, he could not avoid putting
on the veneer of dandified Byronism so prevalent
among society youths in those days. In his case,
most of it was a pose. Yet he was acute enough
to see through the emptiness and futility of the
society in which he lived, its satellite world of
theatrical and ballet stars included. And he came
to despise it the more easily since he himself was
considered a paragon of all its accomplishments.
As a result, he developed that sceptical aloofness
which was bound to turn him into a "superfluous
man" with no real hold upon life. There may
have been a dormant strength in him, potential
goodness and active intelligence; but lacking any
deeper focus or rootedness, all his qualities remained sterile. And what his fashionable romanticism amounted to is clearly indicated by
124

EVGENY ONEGIN

Pushkin in a later chapter (VII, 22) where he speaks of his hero's literary interests:

> 'Twas long, we know, since our Evgeny
> Disliking all his books began;
> Yet there were certain works, not many,
> Which he excluded from his ban:
> The singer of the Giaour and Juan,
> And a romance or two, a new one
> In which the age its face might see,
> And our contemporaries be,
> With some fair share of truth, depicted:
> The soul without morality,
> The temper egoistic, dry
> And in excess to dreams addicted;
> The bitter, angry cast of thought
> A-boil with deeds— that came to naught.

Having become familiar with the glittering foam of life, Onegin felt its aftermath of boredom, which was not quite genuine either, but largely a reflection of his own snobbery. It was in this state of mind that he, like Aleko or the hero of *The Prisoner in the Caucasus*, was suddenly transferred into much simpler surroundings. These were provided by the Russian country-side, where Onegin had inherited his uncle's estate. But the country, however beautiful, was no cure for his *blasé* egotism.

> The country nook that bored Evgeny
> Was just a thing of pure delight
> We should thank heaven for, as any
> Lover of harmless pleasure might.

A hill from all the winds excluded
The master's house; it lay secluded
Above a stream, and far away
Stretched flower-besprinkled meadows gay
With golden fields of harvest blended.
A village twinkled here and there;
Herds roamed the pastures everywhere;
A huge wild garden, too, extended
Its dense and canopying shades,
A haunt for musing Dryad maids.

And here a castle was erected
As castles should be: firmly based,
Quiet, a fabric much respected,
In the old, clever, charming taste.
The rooms were high and many; brocaded
Silks on the parlour walls paraded,
Ancestral portraits also, while
The stoves were shot with many a tile.
Now long had all been antiquated,
I know not rightly why, indeed;
My friend however had small need
Of this; nor cared he if he waited
In ancient or in modish hall;
It mattered not—he yawned in all.

Nor did he feel any better among the provincial
gentry with their out-of-date ideas, their poor
taste and bad manners. The only exception was
the young squire and poet Lensky, just back from
a German University, whence he had

> brought solid fruits of learning
> Away from cloudy Germany,
> And dreamed when all men should be free.

An oddish soul—yet hotly burning;
Enthusiast in talk; and set
Upon his neck were curls of jet.

Quite in the style of the "beautiful soul" (*schoene Seele*) so dear to the German sentimentalists, Lensky represented the Zhukovsky trend in poetry and the enthusiasm of certain Moscow youths, such as the poet Venevitinov, among whom German idealistic philosophy was a cult.[1] Far from being a victory over Onegin's flippancy, his exalted state of mind was only a by-passing of it in order to indulge in naïve wishful thinking. In essence it was even less real than Onegin's pose. As Pushkin puts it,

He sang of parting and of pain;
Of dim horizons,—and again
Of what?—romance, and roses blowing.
He sang of lands, where on the breast
Of peace, of old he long would rest
While, fountain-like, his tears were flowing;
And how life's flower had died unseen;
—This when he had not turned eighteen.

Onegin and Lensky were mutually attracted, not because they shared the same interests and ideas, but by the law of contrast which in the end made them almost indispensable to one another.

At first they bored each other, true,
And incompatibly were mated;

[1] According to one of Pushkin's friends (Pletnyov), Lensky was partly modelled on Pushkin's schoolfellow and subsequent Decembrist, V. Kyukhelbeker.

But then came liking; then would they
Ride out together every day;
And soon could not be separated.
Thus (I too hasten to confess)
Men become friends—through idleness.

Lensky introduced his friend to Mme Larin, a widow whose household was typical of the country-house of that period. One of her two daughters, Olga—a pretty and vivacious but an otherwise ordinary "sweet girl" type—was Lensky's fiancée. Her elder sister, Tatyana or Tanya, though neither vivacious nor pretty, was something different. Pushkin describes her as

—mute, shy and melancholy,
Timid as a woodland hind; and wholly
A stranger lass she seemed to be
In her own house and family.
And never could her sire, or mother,
Win her caress; she did not care
To join the children's mob, or share
Their sports and gambols like another;
But often by the window lay
And said no word, the livelong day.

But such was only Tatyana's surface. Underneath that mask there was a solid character and a capacity for profound affection, which she was willing to bestow only on a person better and different from those she saw around. Her blunder was that on meeting Onegin, so different from her provincial acquaintances, she took him for an exceptional man and, through sheer naïveté,

fell in love with him at first sight. From the third
chapter onward, the "novel" thus becomes the
history of Tatyana's love for Onegin.

III

It goes without saying that Tatyana is the
opposite of Onegin: natural, straightforward and
sincere in whatever she does. She is also rooted in
her native soil—a fact conveyed even by her
Christian name, used until then mainly by
peasants. Pushkin gathered in her some of the
best qualities of the Russian woman, yet without
actually idealising her.[1] Having surrendered
to her new and overwhelming experience, she
tried to discover in Onegin some interest in her,
but in vain. For him Tatyana was just a
provincial girl, exceptional in certain things but
hardly worth any particular notice. She suffered
in silence, and made all sorts of allowances; but
when her despair became unbearable, she com-
mitted a *faux pas* which was itself a proof of her
naïve sincerity. She wrote Onegin a letter
opening with these lines:

"That I am writing you this letter
Will tell you all; and you are free
Now to despise me; and how better,
I wonder, could you punish me?

[1] It is not without interest that, in a letter addressed to Pushkin
at Mikhaylovskoye, A. Rayevsky refers to Tatyana as being a
portrait of Countess Vorontsova, with whom Pushkin had been
in love while in Odessa.

But you, if you are sparing ever
One drop of pity for my fate,
Will not have left me desolate.
I wished at first, believe me, never
To say a word, and then my shame
Had been unknown to you; small blame
Could I have hoped, but once a week
Here, in our village, when you came,
To see you, and to hear you speak,
And pass a single word of greeting,
Think of you only, night and day,
And wait—until another meeting.
You are not sociable, they say;
The solitude, the country, bore you.
We are not smart in any way,
But always had a welcome for you.
Why came you? why to us? Alone,
In this forgotten hamlet hidden,
I never should have known you, known
The bitterness of pangs unbidden."

Onegin did not answer. Yet in his own way he
felt touched by Tatyana's confession of love.
When he called on the Larins again he contrived
to meet her *tête-à-tête*. Partly from politeness and
partly because he meant it, or thought he meant
it, he spoke first of all of her guileless sincerity
which (so he said)

> has stirred in me
> The pulses of long-silenced feeling.
> I would not offer praise; but now
> Will, in repayment, all avow
> In words as artless and revealing.

So hear my shrift; myself and it,
Unto your judgment I submit.

Quite in the style of that other "superfluous man," the hero of *The Prisoner in the Caucasus*, Onegin confessed his inability to love, enjoying as it were his own despondence: "Past years, old dreams, no resurrection can find, nor I my soul renew." And as for marriage ties, the mere idea was enough to make him shudder.

"I was not made for joy; my spirit
Is alien to that blissful lot;
All the perfections you inherit
Are useless; I deserve them not.
For us—and take my word's assurance—
Marriage were torment, past endurance.
However strong my love may be,
Custom will quench it, speedily."

After a homily on the kind of inexperience which often "leads to grief" he left her humiliated, crushed. Meanwhile, Onegin's exasperation with his provincial neighbours (whom he insultingly avoided) was on the increase. Once, in the winter, he gave in to Lensky's entreaties and called on the Larins. It was Tatyana's name-day. The sight of Onegin distressed Tatyana. Annoyed by her badly concealed misery, and even more by the collection of country squires present, Onegin was so angry with Lensky for having dragged him there that he decided to punish him by deliberately flirting with Olga during the ball.

131

Olga was so flattered that she neglected the much too excitable Lensky, who in the end challenged his friend to a duel. Bored by it all, Onegin thought of smoothing the affair over, but certain unexpected trifles, as well as the fear of public opinion, compelled him to accept the challenge. The duel took place, and Lensky was killed, fortunately young, i.e. before he had had time to pass through the usual routine of mutations and disappointments involved by life.

He might have greatly changed and married;
No longer with the Muses tarried;
And, happy in the country, worn
His quilted dressing-gown—and horn;
He would have known what life is truly;
At forty would have had the gout,
Drunk, fed, moped, pined, with fat swelled out;
At last, and in his bed, would duly,
While doctors gazed, and women cried,
With all his children round—have died.

After the duel Onegin hastily departed, and like another Childe Harold began roaming all over the country. Olga soon forgot her poet and married a smart lancer. Tatyana at first resigned herself to loneliness. Unable to drive Onegin from her mind, she paid a visit to his locked-up house. The kindly caretaker showed her the apartments which still bore the imprint of Onegin's habits. Somewhat puzzled by what she saw, Tatyana repeated her visits, and gradually calmed down; for now she began to suspect that all the time she had been in love with a phantom, with her idea of Onegin rather than with the real man. Having become to some extent familiar with his tastes and with the books in his library, she wondered whether he was not perhaps a "grievous, dangerous freak,"

> an imitation,
> A phantom nothing; or, at best,
> Moscow, in Harold's mantle drest,
> Of foreign whims an illustration?
> A modish phrase-book, rich in store?
> Nay, a sheer parody, no more?

A clue to him may perhaps be provided by this anonymous epigraph in French with which Pushkin prefaced as it were the "novel": *Pétri de vanité il avait encore plus de cette espèce d'orgueil qui fait avouer avec la même indifférence les bonnes comme les mauvaises actions, suite d'un sentiment de supériorité peut-être imaginaire.* (Infected with vanity, he suffered even more from that kind of conceit which makes one display with the same indifference both one's good and evil actions—the result of a feeling of perhaps imaginary superiority.) But here we leave both Tatyana and Onegin in order to meet them again in entirely different circumstances.

IV

After a few years the action is transferred once more to Petersburg. Onegin has just returned from his travels. He is taken to a fashionable ball, and among the guests suddenly recognises Tatyana, now married to an elderly dignitary and enjoying all the adulation due to her new position in life. The naïve and provincial Tanya, to whom he had once sermonised on self-control, is now a mature, resplendent beauty adored by the *grand monde*! When he is formally introduced to her, she calmly

> Regards Onegin. . . . None the less,
> Whate'er embarrassment dismayed her,
> Whatever shock her soul might feel,
> Whate'er astonishment conceal,
> Yet there was nothing that betrayed her;
> The same high breeding still she wore
> And bowed, as tranquil as before.

The pattern of the plot is repeated, but the rôles are reversed. Now it is Onegin who falls in love with Tatyana.

> Daily her stairway he approaches,
> Her entrance-hall, her window-pane,
> A dogging shadow in her train.

As once she wrote to him, he now writes to her a confession of love.

> "I well foresee how this confession
> Of my sad secret will offend;
> What haughty glances you will bend;
> How bitter, scornful their expression.

What seek I? What can be my quest
In thus my inmost soul revealing?
Perhaps I only shall suggest
Some joyful, some malicious feeling."

This time it is Tatyana who remains silent.
He writes again, but there is no answer. Driven
to despair, Onegin rushes one morning into her
house, where he finds her alone, poring over his
letter, her face stained with tears. Overwhelmed,
he seizes her hand and falls on his knees. Tatyana

Her gaze upon Onegin set
With no surprise, no indignation.
His ailing, his extinguished look,
Beseeching air, and dumb rebuke
She marked; like some reincarnation
Of that once simple maid she seems,
With her young heart, her early dreams.

Underneath her splendour and her aristocratic
polish Tatyana was still the same simple and
serious Tanya he had known in the country.
Even the false glitter of society was unable to
harm her true self.

"This pomp, which all in tinsel dresses
The life that I abhor so much;
My evenings, stylish house, successes
In the world's eddy—what are such
To me, Onegin? I'd surrender
Gladly, this minute, all the splendour,
Glitter and vapour, noise, parade,
For our poor house, and garden by it
Left wild, and bookshelf; for that place
Where first I saw Onegin's face."

But she now looked differently upon Onegin. Having sized him up during the sad days after his departure, she knew that he had repudiated her love out of vanity, and that now too it was largely vanity (unconscious perhaps) that had made him fall in love with her.

> "Why mark me down—is this the reason,—
> That I must figure, in due season,
> In these high circles? that to-day
> I'm rich, and notable they say,
> And have a husband maimed in fighting,
> And so we are caressed at Court?
> That all would notice and report
> Disgrace or shame, of my inviting?
> And, with the world, there might accrue
> A tempting honour—unto you?"

These reproaches are uttered by a self-possessed woman who knows that Onegin is a "parody." Yet the tenderness of her first love, however misplaced, is still there. Frankly and without any sentimentality she acknowledges:

> "I love you (why sophisticate it?)
> But I'm another's pledged; and I
> To him stay constant, till I die."

Whereupon the hero and the heroine part, presumably for ever. As though dissatisfied with this ending, Pushkin in September 1835 wrote two stanzas as a tentative continuation. Earlier he had thought of rounding off the "novel" by letting Onegin die in the Caucasus, or else join

the Decembrists, which actually happened in the
tenth chapter written in cipher and subsequently
burnt. The few fragments left (describing the
gatherings of the prospective Decembrists) contain
such scathing remarks about Alexander I that
one ceases to wonder at Pushkin's safety-measure.
Finally, the "novel" was left as it stood: inconclusive and at the same time as organic and convincing as life itself.

> And happy he who, early quitting
> Life's feast, has not the dregs drunk up
> Of the wine brimming in the cup,
> To read life's story still omitting,
> —And takes his leave—abruptly, too,
> As I with my Onegin do.

V

Evgeny Onegin is supposed to have been planned
on a bigger scale. It was to consist of three parts,
the first of which would have comprised chapters
I–VI of the version we know. During the process
of writing, Pushkin condensed the material to
nine, and then (by deleting Onegin's travels)
to eight chapters. Such an alteration of the
original plan may perhaps account for one or two
minor gaps in the "novel." Tatyana's transition
from a shy provincial girl to a brilliant society
woman, for example, is rather sudden. Yet the
reader, learning what happened during her stay
at Moscow, soon recognises that old Tatyana

even in her resplendent new rôle and position. On the other hand, the *dénouement* of *Onegin* may also have been prompted by certain personal reasons.

Tatyana's attitude towards her husband somewhat resembled that of Natalia towards Pushkin. Her dignified simplicity represented the social aspect, and her loyalty the kind of moral ideal Pushkin wanted to find in his future wife. Perhaps we ought to add that Tatyana with her elderly husband reminds one of Maria Rayevskaya, who married the much older Prince Sergey Volkonsky and (after the December rising) followed him to Siberia from a sense of loyalty and duty rather than from love.[1] For other autobiographical elements in the "novel" one could for instance point to Tatyana's lovable old nurse, a portrait of Arina. Onegin's experiences in the first chapter are largely those of Pushkin himself during his Petersburg period, between 1817 and 1820. The rural scenes again were drawn by Pushkin from life. In a letter to Vyazemsky he says: "In the fourth canto of *Onegin* I depicted my own life." Many a wonderful landscape impression must have been inspired by the environs of Mikhaylovskoye. Nor must we overlook the fact that after the inimitable humorous inflection of some earlier chapters, the last chapter, completed at Boldino, is serious in tone and as if reflecting

[1] She figures among those wives who voluntarily joined their Decembrist husbands in Siberia and were later celebrated in the poetic series, *Russian Women*, by N. Nekrasov

Pushkin's own moods on the eve of his marriage.

Yet whatever personal elements there may be in this work, they are all wonderfully transmuted and blended with its objective side, which the critic Belinsky described as an "encyclopædia of Russian life" and a "poetic picture of Russian society during one of the most interesting phases of its development." Here, if anywhere, Pushkin showed all his descriptive and plastic power, as well as his capacity for rendering character by means of suggestive lyrical "atmosphere." It was through *Onegin* that he squared his accounts with Byron and the romantic movement. Having started his "novel" at the height of his own Byronic period, Pushkin gradually pronounced in it a double verdict on romanticism. Tatyana's summing up of Onegin as a parody was one of them, while the other was indicated in Pushkin's bantering attitude towards Lensky (a product of the German romantic movement with its quietist or reactionary feudal-medieval propensities, so dear to the Holy Alliance). Further, *Evgeny Onegin* expresses Pushkin's philosophy of the acceptance of life, a philosophy not so much of happiness as of a balanced serenity on the part of a man who has learned both the value and the price of things in our bewildering world. Last but not least, this masterpiece became one of the corner-stones of Russian literature after Pushkin.

Chapter Seven

Pushkin and Shakespeare

I

AS early as 1822 Pushkin acknowledged the growing influence of English literature in Russia, and welcomed it as a more vitalising factor than the currents which came from France. His own indebtedness was by no means confined to Byron alone. If his southern period was marked by Byron's influence, his stay at Mikhaylovskoye coincided with his interest in Shakespeare, which —coupled with Pushkin's study of Russian history—resulted in the first Shakespearean play of merit in Russian literature: *Boris Godunov*. It was with the help of Shakespeare that Pushkin freed himself from Byronism and made use of certain new elements which were likely to foster his own artistic growth—this time in the direction of the drama.

It should be borne in mind that Russian dramatic literature was still poor in the days when Pushkin thought of grafting Shakespeare's influence upon it. Dating from the second half of the seventeenth century, when Simeon Polotsky modelled his dramatised biblical parables on the Jesuit school-plays of the period, Russian drama developed slowly and under Western guidance. Its eighteenth-century character was under the spell of French classicism. The later middle-class drama, or what passed as such, received its impetus from Beaumarchais and Sébastien Mercier, while Rousseau's *Le devin du village* may have fostered an interest in comic plays (with music) from folk-life. Nor was Shakespeare entirely absent from the Russian stage. The eighteenth-century dramatist Sumarokov went so far as to "adapt" *Hamlet* to the Procrustean bed of pseudo-classic tradition and to give the play a respectable happy ending. He married Ophelia to the melancholy prince, whom after all her trials she piously exhorts:

> Go, my prince, into the temple,
> Show thyself to the people.
> And I will go and pay
> My last duty to my dead.

This curious travesty written in Alexandrine couplets and with the three unities triumphant, appeared in 1748 and was produced two years later. Sumarokov wrote also his *Dimitry the Usurper* (the theme which Pushkin took up later in *Boris Godunov*) at least with a vague idea of Shakespeare's historical plays. Catherine II herself paraphrased, rather freely and with Russian local colour, *The Merry Wives of Windsor*, and also *Timon of Athens*—under the title *The*

Wastrel.[1] Karamzin was responsible for the first Russian translation of *Julius Caesar* (1787), in the preface to which he stated with genuine enthusiasm that "few authors have penetrated so deeply into human nature as Shakespeare. Few have gauged so well the most secret springs of every single passion, temperament and way of life as this marvellous artist. . . . His plays are as full of diversity as the immense theatre of Nature itself." The budding romantics of the 1820's combined their appreciation of German idealistic philosophy (especially of Schelling and Hegel) with a growing admiration for Shakespeare. This was particularly true of the circle gathering round the young Moscow poet D. V. Venevitinov (1805–27). The pioneering essay *On Romantic Poetry* (1823) by a certain Orest Somov, a lesser Byronic poet, was a panegyric of Shakespeare's work. Yet it was Pushkin, once again, who emulated Shakespeare with skill and understanding. He transferred his allegiance from Byron to Shakespeare some time in 1824, and in July 1825 he wrote to N. N. Rayevsky: "I have read neither Calderon nor Vega, but what a man this Shakespeare is! I

[1] The earliest Russian translation from Shakespeare, a fragment (V, 3) from *Romeo and Juliet*, appeared in 1772. The first play to be completely translated (in 1783) was *Richard III*. A version of *Othello*, done chiefly from the mutilated and sentimentalised French adaptation by Ducis, was performed in 1806. It had a happy ending with virtue duly rewarded. So had *King Lear*, produced in the following year. The first performance of Shakespeare's (not Sumarokov's) *Hamlet* on the Russian stage took place in 1810.

am simply overwhelmed! How petty Byron the tragedian looks if compared with him, the same Byron who *in summa* understood one character only. Byron simply divided his own personality among his heroes: one of them he endowed with his own pride, another with his hatred, a third with his melancholy, and so on. In this manner he created out of one complete sombre yet energetic character a number of insignificant characters. This, however, is not really tragedy." Nor did Pushkin's interest in Shakespeare ever diminish as did his interest in Byron. On the contrary, he kept deepening his knowledge of Shakespeare's plays and methods, as we can see from his later comparison between Molière and Shakespeare.

"The characters created by Shakespeare," he says in an illuminating remark, "are not, like those of Molière, types of such-and-such a passion or such-and-such a vice: they are living beings with many passions and many vices. Their various qualities are developed before the spectator by the circumstances which confront them. Molière's miser is miserly, and that is all; Shakespeare's Shylock is miserly, sagacious, vindictive, fond of his child, and sharp-witted. With Molière the hypocrite is hypocritical, no matter whether he runs after his benefactor's daughter or merely asks for a glass of water. Shakespeare's hypocrite, on the other hand, passes legal judgment with conceited severity,

143

but justly; he justifies his cruelty with the careful reasoning of a public man; he seduces the innocent with powerful, captivating sophistry, and not with a ludicrous jumble of piety and lovemaking. Angelo is a hypocrite because his public actions contradict his secret passions. And what depth there is in this character! But nowhere, perhaps, is Shakespeare's versatile genius reflected with such multiformity as in Falstaff, whose vices are linked one with another like the performers of an ancient bacchanalian chain-dance. If we analyse the character of Falstaff we see that its chief ingredient is sensuality. From his youth onwards his first care was probably coarse, cheap adventure; but after fifty he grew fat and senile, gluttony and wine markedly taking the upper hand over Venus. He is, in the second place, a coward, but having spent his life with young scapegraces, constantly subjected to their jibes and pranks, he conceals his cowardice behind a brazen audacity both evasive and ironical. Habitually and calculatedly boastful, Falstaff is no fool. On the contrary, he has acquired quite a few of the habits of a man used to good society. Of principles he has none. He is as weak as a woman. He needs strong Spanish wine, rich food, money for his mistresses; and to obtain these he is ready for anything except downright danger."

II

The somewhat shadowy figures typical of Pushkin's Byronic period gave way to solid three-dimensional characters soon after his acquaintanceship with Shakespeare's works. These also stimulated an interest in the theatre and the drama which was not new to him. As a boy Pushkin paid frequent visits (in the company of his father) to Prince Yusupov's private serf-theatre in Moscow, at a time when he was reading Molière and had even imitated him in a lost comedy written in French under the title *L'escamoteur*. There were theatricals at the Lycée. Onegin's contacts with theatres, their fans and their *divae*, as described in the first chapter of *Evgeny Onegin*, were based on Pushkin's own experiences during his Petersburg period. While he was in the south, both *Ruslan and Ludmila* and *The Prisoner in the Caucasus* were turned into ballets and had under the guidance of the once famous Didelot a great success in Petersburg and Moscow. At the same time, his *Fountain of Bakhchisaray* was remade into a play, *Kherim Ghirey*, by the prolific dramatist Prince A. A. Shakhovskoy.

What drew Pushkin's particular attention to the Russian theatre during the 'twenties was however its bad state. True enough, *Hamlet*, *Othello*, *Macbeth*, *King Lear* and *The Tempest* figured among its productions, but on the whole the repertory in both Russian capitals was far from

inspiring.[1] Its bulk consisted of translated plays—
often remade so as to suit the Russian tastes.
Pseudo-classical tragedies by Ozerov and Knyazhnin were still in favour, partly because of a lack
of new plays, and partly owing to the interpre-
tation of "classical" heroines by the matchless
actress Semyonova. Cheap comedies or melo-
dramas by the German playwright Kotzebue
enjoyed, until the end of the 'twenties, an unqualified success. So did the declamatory historical drama with a patriotic and often reactionary halo. The two purveyors of such plays,
Zotov and Shakhovskoy, paid ample tribute to
official patriotism; but as they were anxious to
make their plays accessible to the masses, both of
them had to abandon the conventions of the stiff
classical form. Some of the younger authors
(Katenin, Kyukhelbeker, Griboyedov) still adhered to the classical pattern and often made use
of it for themes of a social or political character—
wisely camouflaged by the ancient Greek garb.
Pushkin himself had started (in 1822) a pseudo-
classic historical tragedy, *Vadim*, which was to be
a disguised attack on autocracy, but gave it up.
Three years later he resumed his dramatic
activities on a different scale, and with the
technical knowledge he had meanwhile gleaned

---

[1] Shakespeare came into his own in Russia only in the 'thirties
of the last century, and this was due chiefly to the superb acting
of some of the principal parts, notably Hamlet, by V. Karatygin
in Petersburg and P. Mochalov in Moscow. By that time more
reliable translations, too, were available.

from Shakespeare. The result was *Boris Godunov*—a play first mentioned by Pushkin in a letter to Vyazemsky on July 13th, 1825, and finished in November in the same year.

There were several other works besides Shakespeare's chronicle-plays that were responsible for it; especially August Schlegel's *Course of Lectures on Dramatic Art and Literature* (a kind of apology for the romantic drama), Karamzin's *History of the Russian State*, and old Russian annals. The broadness of the canvas was provided by the agitated events of history. The dramatic form and treatment of those events were however modelled on Shakespeare, whose plays were—in Pushkin's opinion—plays for the people in the wider sense, as distinct from classical French drama written primarily for the Court. He eliminated everything artificial in the name of that naturalness which he had learned from Shakespeare. "I followed Shakespeare," he says, "in his broad and free treatment of character, in his incomparable choice of types, and in his simplicity. From Karamzin I took the methodical course of events; and in the old annals I tried to discover the mentality as well as the language of the epoch."

III

The course of events referred to is the "time of troubles" at the end of the sixteenth and the beginning of the seventeenth century (roughly between 1595 and 1605), when Russia was in the throes of political and social chaos. Soon after the death of Ivan the Terrible his little son Dimitry (Demetrius) was murdered. The murder was generally attributed to Boris Godunov, Ivan's ambitious son-in-law and subsequent ruler of Russia.[1] While Boris was on the throne, a runaway monk, Grishka Otrepyev, escaped to Poland, where he pretended to be Dimitry miraculously saved from being murdered. The Poles welcomed him. Always willing to foment trouble in Russia, they equipped the would-be Dimitry with an army and sent him against Moscow. Adroit and sagacious, the Pretender relied on the dissatisfaction of the masses, whom he expected to turn against Boris. In the end he occupied Moscow, where he ruled for a while together with his Polish wife Marina, until he too was assassinated. The country began to quieten down only after the election of the first Romanov to the throne, in 1613.

These events proved dramatic enough to draw the attention of Europe, where the interest in Russia had much increased since Richard Chancellor's landing in the region of Archangel in 1553. In the seventeenth century it was, in fact, so great that Milton himself thought it worth his while to write a *History of Moscovia*. But even

---

[1] This view, held by Karamzin, was contested at least by two other historians: Polevoy and Pogodin.

before Milton's birth there appeared a number of books on Russia, among which Dr. Giles Fletcher's work, *Of the Russe Commonwealth, or Manner of Government by the Russe Emperor (commonly called the Emperor of Moscouia)*, 1591, aimed at giving a wider knowledge of that country to English readers. His nephew, the dramatist John Fletcher, must have been familiar with it when writing his play, *The Loyal Subject* (1618). He took the plot from one of Bandello's stories, but transferred the action to Moscow—with Burris, "an honest lord, the Duke's favourite," as one of the chief characters. There is little doubt that the name Burris was but a distorted version of Boris Godunov. In Spain the action of Calderon's play, *Afectos de Odio y Amor*, takes place partly in Russia, and the Duke of Russia, Casimiro, is one of the characters. Another play, *El Gran Duque de Moscovia y Emperador Perseguido*, this time by Lope de Vega, brings us, however, right to the "troubled" period with the Pretender Dimitry as its hero.

As the usurper-theme seems to have particularly appealed to Western littérateurs at a time when the "divine right of kings" was in question, the figure of Dimitry continued to stir the imaginations long after the troubles caused by him were over. An opera under the title *Demetrio* was performed in Venice in 1660. In England a play (unfinished) about the Russian Pretender was written by Richard Cumberland at the end of the eighteenth century, whereas a dramatic sketch on the same theme, *Dimitry* by G. G. Alexander, appeared as late as 1829. Literary interest in the false Dimitry was however strongest in Germany, where it persisted until our days. ·Schiller, Kotzebue, Bodenstedt, Hebbel and some later dramatists took up the theme, Schiller's unfinished *Demetrius* being by far the best. Also the poet F. M. R. Lenz, of "Storm and Stress" (*Sturm und Drang*) fame, who spent his last years in Moscow and was in contact with Russian authors, left fragments of a drama about Boris Godunov. In Russia, Sumarokov's *Dimitry the Usurper* dates from 1771. So Pushkin was by no means the first to tackle the subject, but he tackled it only after a careful perusal of Shakespeare's *Richard III, Henry IV, Henry V* and also *King John*. Having decided to write a similar chronicle-play, but rooted in Russian soil and history, Pushkin adopted the "broad manner" of Shakespeare and divided the play itself into twenty-five scenes, two of which he subsequently deleted. This is how he explains his method in the draft of a letter to N. N. Rayevsky (1827): "Firmly convinced that the antiquated forms of our theatre need reshaping, I constructed my tragedy according to the system of our father Shakespeare, and having sacrificed to him the first two classical unities I scarcely retained the third. The time-honoured Alexandrine I replaced by five-footed blank verse, and in some scenes I even condescended to use despised prose; in a word, I wrote a truly romantic tragedy."

The word "romantic" stands here for Shakespearean—with certain reservations. Quite in tune with Karamzin, Godunov is put forward (whether rightly or wrongly) as the murderer of the Tsarevich, and this crime becomes his tragic guilt, as well as his fate. Realising that he, too, is a usurper he falls a prey to his own doubt, fear and suspicion, while the false Dimitry looms nearer and nearer like a kind of Nemesis: inexorable and final. This basic mood keeps growing until it reaches its climax in the Tsar's death, which is followed by the murder of his children at the moment Dimitry is on the point of becoming the master of Moscow. Yet it would be wrong to see in *Boris Godunov* only a psychological theme. The play, with its variety of scenes and characters, develops on two planes. One of them is psychological, and the other— broadly speaking—political. The first is represented by the inner drama of Boris, while the second merges with the historical background. The play has been described as a social-political tragedy, and Pushkin himself wrote to Vyazemsky in September 1825: "I look upon him (Boris) from a political standpoint without paying attention to the poetic side."

Boris Godunov is certainly less brilliant with regard to its "poetic side" than Schiller's *Demetrius*, for example. It is also less agitated, less rich in passion than Shakespeare's plays. But this toning down was due to Pushkin's tendency to make his characters speak as simply and naturally as they would in real life. "Convincingness of situations and naturalness of the dialogue"—this was what Pushkin demanded from a play, and he kept to this rule even at the risk of appearing bald in comparison with his chief model, Shakespeare. The five-footed iambic line used by him made a return to the solemn declamatory Alexandrine quite impossible. Several scenes are in ordinary conversational prose. And instead of the strict unity of time and place there is a fairly loose sequence of episodes, each of them as it were with its own climax.

In spite of the title it is not Godunov but Dimitry who dominates the stage and provides the focus unifying the play. From a dramatic standpoint Dimitry is the most articulate of all the characters presented. While Godunov necessarily remains in one prevailing mood, Dimitry is shown in a variety of moods, although he has no definite political line except that of dexterously exploiting the circumstances. It is known that the Poles had their own reasons for aiding and equipping the Pretender. So had the Jesuits around him, who hoped to fish in troubled waters. Yet Dimitry's final success was made possible only by the support of the dissatisfied masses. Unstable and changing though they were, they had joined him and in the end became the de-

I have seen knights and many a noble count.
Think you I coldly spurned their humble prayers
Only to yield me to a truant monk?

PRETENDER (*rising*):
Look not with scorn upon the young pretender.
In him lie hidden virtues, it may be
Worthy to gain the royal throne of Moscow,
Yes, even worthy of your priceless hand.

MARINA: Worthy of the hangman's noose; insolent
wretch.

PRETENDER: I am to blame; for, blinded by my
pride,
I have deceived both God and kings, have lied
To all men; but it befits you not, Marina,
To punish me. I have told the truth to you.
No, I could not go on deceiving you:
For me you were the only sacred being
Before whom I dared not dissimulate.
Love, only love, jealous and blind compelled me
To tell you all.

MARINA: Why boast of that, you madman?
Who bade you to confess your faults to me?
If you, a nameless vagrant, have already
Miraculously hoodwinked two great nations,
Then at the very least it is your duty
To prove you're worthy of your high success,
And put a seal upon your daring fraud
By deep, persistent, lasting secrecy.
Say then, can I yield myself to you?
Can I, forgetting birth and maiden shame,
Unite my destiny to yours, when you
Yourself with such simplicity of soul
So lightly can reveal your shameful secret?
Out of pure love, he says, he blabbed to me!
I marvel that, till now, you have not published

Your tale out of pure friendship to my father,
Or to our lord the king out of pure joy,
Or to Prince Wishniowetski out of ardent
Zeal of a true and faithful servitor.

PRETENDER: I swear to you that you and you alone
Have power to constrain my heart's confession.
I swear to you that never, anywhere,
Not at the feast amid wine's heady fumes,
Not in the sacred tie of friendship's talk,
No, not beneath the knife, or on the rack
Shall my tongue render up these weighty secrets.

MARINA: You swear! O then it seems I must
    believe. . . .
O I believe you, but may I know by what
You swear? Is it not by God, as best befits
The Jesuits' devout adopted child?
Or, perhaps, simply by your royal word
Like a king's son? Is it not so? Tell me. . . .

PRETENDER: The shade of John the Dread [1]
    adopted me;
Out of the tomb he christened me Dimitry;
He has stirred up the nations around about me
And has appointed Boris as my victim.
I am Tsarevitch! Enough. I am ashamed
To bow my head to a proud Polish girl.
Good-bye forever. Now war's bloody game,
My destiny with wide-embracing cares
Will stifle all the pangs of love, I hope.
O how I shall detest your very name,
When once the heat of passion has been spent!
Now I shall leave you. Ruin or a crown
Are waiting now for me on Russia's plains.
Whether I meet a soldier's death in battle,

---

[1] I.e. Ivan the Terrible.

Or like a miscreant on a public scaffold,
You shall not be my comrade or my helpmate,
You shall not share my destiny with me.
But it may be one day you will regret
The fate which now you scornfully reject.

MARINA: But what if I forestall you and expose
Your daring fraud and publish it to all?

PRETENDER: And do you think I am afraid of you?
Will men believe a Polish girl before me,
The Tsarevitch of Russia? You must know
That neither king nor pope nor barons trouble
Their heads about the truth of my pretensions.
If I am Dimitry or not, what do they care?
But I am a pretext for disputes and war
That is all they need; and as for you, fair rebel,
Believe me they will make you hold your tongue.
Farewell.

MARINA: Tsarevitch, stay! For now at last
I do not hear a boy's speech but a man's.
Prince, it has reconciled my heart to you.
Your senseless outburst I can now forget.
I see Dimitry now again. But listen,
The time has come, awake, delay no more,
So quickly lead your army on to Moscow,
The Kremlin purge, sit on the Russian throne,
Then send your nuptial embassy to me.
But, as God hears me, know, until your foot
Treads on the step that leads up to the throne,
Till Godunov is vanquished by your hand,
I'll listen to no word of love from you.

If Boris has one or two features in common
with Richard III, Dimitry resembles, as Pushkin
himself has pointed out in one of his remarks,

another Henry—Henri Quatre of France. "Like him, Dimitry is brave, generous and bragging; both are indifferent to religion, since both change it for political reasons; both are fond of pleasure and of war; both are carried away by utopian projects and become centres of plots." Boris and Dimitry never meet face to face. This may seem a drawback from a dramatic point of view, yet strangely enough it does not diminish the tension of the conflict itself, which is shown from such an angle as to keep us wondering which of the two, Dimitry or Boris, is the actual usurper. Technically, each scene gives the impression of a self-contained or almost self-contained unit, while yet building up the play as a whole. And the various layers of Russian society are shown with that disciplined realism in which pathos is balanced by humour and where art intensifies life itself.

V

In 1829 Pushkin remarked (in a draft) that the success or failure of *Boris Godunov* would affect the "entire dramatic system" of his country. When read privately by Pushkin himself in various literary circles, the play had an enthusiastic reception. The poets Vyazemsky and Baratynsky, the great Pole Mickiewicz (who heard it in 1828), as well as a few other discriminating minds, were most appreciative. But here its success ended.

Quite apart from the misunderstandings he had
with the Tsar and the censorship, the play when
published was coldly received by the public and
by the majority of the critics.[1] This may perhaps
explain why Pushkin gave up any further experiments along Shakespearean lines, although, judging by his letter to N. N. Rayevsky in 1829, he
had intended to write a series of chronicle-plays,
with the various characters from *Boris Godunov*
alternately taking the principal parts in them.
Nor did Pushkin's contact with Shakespeare end
with this play. There are some indications that
he hoped, or that he even tried, to translate
Measure for Measure. But he preferred to transpose
it instead, with some alterations, into a narrative
poem under the title *Angelo* (1833). In doing so
he took from Shakespeare only the *motif*, which
he condensed into a quiet poem written in
Alexandrine verse. He also reduced Shakespeare's
twenty-five characters to nine, and gave the plot
a happy ending imbued with humanitarian sentiment. *Angelo*, uneven though it may be, is
another illustration of Pushkin's enviable capacity
for making use of other poet's themes, not in
order to adapt himself to them but to adapt them
to himself, that is, to transform them in his own
image. In this case it even implied a certain
rivalry on his part with Molière's Tartuffe.
Further examples can be found in the "little

[1] Its first performance took place in 1870: forty-five years
after it had been written. Due justice was given to it only after
the revolution of 1917.

tragedies" which he wrote at Boldino in the autumn of 1830. If in *Boris Godunov* he made Shakespeare his starting-point, he turned in these to themes and characters previously worked out by some other poets or dramatists. And again he made use of them not in order to repeat what had already been said, but to show them in a new light, and from a new angle. This is why his four dramatic miniatures deserve special study.

Chapter Eight

Pushkin's "Little Tragedies"

I

THE idea of writing a series of short "tabloid" plays came to Pushkin in July 1826, or perhaps even earlier if we are to judge by his *Scene from Faust* (1825). Originally he jotted down the following ten titles for this purpose: *The Miser; Romulus and Remus; Mozart and Salieri; Don Juan; Jesus; Berald of Savoy; Paul I; The Enamoured Devil; Dimitry and Marina; Kurbsky*. Most of the titles are suggestive of big and complex themes, which would demand unusual concentration if treated within the small compass aimed at by Pushkin. He finished only three of the intended ten plays—*The Miser Knight* (*The Miser*), *The Stone Guest* (*Don Juan*) and *Mozart and Salieri*—all of which are among the most condensed things Pushkin ever wrote.

What surprises one in the list itself, short though it be, is the variety of the themes. Three of them, *Dimitry and Marina*, *Kurbsky*, and *Paul I*, are taken from Russian history. *Dimitry and Marina* would have linked the series to *Boris Godunov*. *Kurbsky* would probably have brought forward the enigmatic personality of Ivan the Terrible, whose despotism found in the boyar Kurbsky an intelligent and formidable opponent. (Kurbsky's son, incidentally, figures in *Boris Godunov*.) *Paul I*, on the other hand, promised to be of topical interest, since that semi-mad "Russian Caligula" was murdered with the knowledge and perhaps the connivance of his own son—the subsequent Tsar Alexander I. Other themes were to deal with passions or obsessions of general human significance, and Pushkin was not deterred by the fact that they had already been treated by a number of important European authors before him. On the contrary, it was through such general themes that he hoped to affiliate all the more closely his native literature with the literary tradition of the West, while showing at the same time the themes themselves in a new and original light.

He must already have contemplated something similar in his brilliant *Scene from Faust*. Pushkin's Faust is not a titanic character but a paranoiac, utterly disappointed with his new knowledge and more depressed by his regained youth than he had been by his old age before his deal with Mephistopheles. As if reluctant to compete with Goethe on his own ground, Pushkin turned to such traditional motives as avarice (*The Miser Knight*), carnal lust (*The Stone Guest*), and envy (*Mozart and Salieri*), which he endeavoured to show as far as possible from an original angle, and with the greatest artistic discipline at his disposal.

This time, too, he was helped by his contact with English literature. As it happened, in 1829 there appeared in Paris a bulky volume, *The Poetic Works of Milman, Bowles, Wilson and Barry Cornwall*, published by A. and W. Galignani. On reading it, Pushkin saw in Barry Cornwall's concise *Dramatic Scenes* something similar to what he himself had been aiming at. Impressed by them, as well as by the English author's determination—stressed in the preface—to write in a "more natural style than that which has for a long time prevailed in our dramatic literature," he modelled, partly at least, his own miniature plays on the dramatic form used by Barry Cornwall.[1] It is also significant that one of his own plays, *The Miser Knight*, he gave out as a Russian version of scenes from a tragi-comedy— *The Covetous Knight*—by the English author Chenstone (*sic!*), which was of course deliberate mystification. He increased the number of his "little tragedies" by *A Feast at the Time of Plague* —his translation of a scene from John Wilson's *A City of the Plague* (1816), printed in the same Galignani volume. Pushkin took only the fourth scene (or most of it) of the first act, but modified its basic mood of pessimism and despair into one of defiance in the teeth of death itself. This is

[1] In his last letter, written on the day of his duel, Pushkin was asking a certain authoress (A. Ishimova) to translate some of Barry Cornwall's *Dramatic Scenes*. She translated them, and they were later printed in *The Contemporary*—the journal founded by Pushkin.

made particularly clear by the interpolation of two songs of his own, one of them being the partly quoted, "War knows the dizziness of drink." The translation bears of course Pushkin's touch, and his blank verse is throughout so simple and at the same time powerful that the scene, taken from a forgotten English play, became paradoxically enough a masterpiece of Russian literature. And lastly, it should be pointed out that in spite of the brevity of his "little tragedies," Pushkin succeeded in avoiding the schematised presentation of characters according to the pseudo-classic canon, which demands that each character should embody one feature only. He endowed them instead with several contradictory features and with something of that inner complexity which he had learned from "our father Shakespeare."

II

The shortest of Pushkin's dramatic miniatures is *Mozart and Salieri*. It consists of two scenes only, some 235 lines, which are packed with content. Pushkin made use of the legend that Mozart had been poisoned by his friend and one-time rival Salieri, to which he added also that about Mozart's famous *Requiem*. The strange rumour concerning Mozart's death was current in those days and found its way into literature, but has been discredited since. Pushkin, an ardent admirer of Mozart, was interested in the hidden inner motives of a crime such as that attributed to Salieri, and set out to explore it.

In confronting Mozart with Salieri, he showed above all the contrast as well as the eternal antagonism between genius and mere talent. There was nothing new in this contrast. The romantics, especially those influenced by Wackenroder, were familiar with it. A Russian translation of Wackenroder's once famous book, *On Art and Artists*, appeared in 1826, and some traces of it can be felt in Salieri's monologue. Pushkin's Salieri is an industrious craftsman, fanatically devoted to music and at the same time devoid of true creative power. So he is doomed to remain a solemn plodder who cannot grasp how it is that the greatest creative genius should have been bestowed on the carefree, childishly irresponsible "idle frivoller" Mozart,[1] and not upon himself as a reward for all his zeal and toil. He listens with amazement to Mozart's music, but the more he is compelled to admire it the more he feels the smart of some injustice which is beyond man's ken. On this plane, Salieri's attitude transcends mere envy; it is tragic and at the same time unanswerable. Hence the conflicting feelings preying upon him, and expressed in the monologue with which the play opens:

[1] There can be no doubt that the "frivoller" Mozart is a transposed portrait of Pushkin himself.

They say there is no justice in the world,
But there is none even in heaven above!
It's all as simple as the scale of C.
I must have been *born* with a love for Art,
For as an infant, in our village church,
I listened to the organ, and hot tears,
Sweet and involuntary tears, gushed out.
The toys and games of childhood I despised,
And lessons, all but music. Firm of purpose
I threw all else aside, and gave my heart
Alone to music. Though the early steps
Were hard, the track, for many a weary month
Tedious, yet I strove and overcame,
Making of toil a stepping-stone to Art;
And I turned craftsman, taught the docile fingers
A quick obedience to the ear. Meanwhile
The notes lay dead, and I dissected music
As 'twere a corpse, and yielded harmony
To algebra. And so at last I ventured
And claimed the prize, surrendering my heart
To rapture of triumphant fantasy.
Not bold enough as yet to think of fame,
I would compose, create, in secrecy,
And often after days of lonely toil,
Neglecting food and rest, but relishing
The ecstasy of tears and inspiration.
I burnt all I had written, coldly gazing
While thought and sound, and image, born of me,
Flamed up and perished in a pallid smoke.
Nay, more—when Gluck appeared, revealing to us
Things deep and strange, to captivate the soul,
Did I not straightway fling the past aside
And all I loved, all I had long believed,
To follow him unquestioning? Like a man
Strayed from his course, but warned, who turns aside

Along a path unknown. At last, I too
Climbing the topless steep of Art attained
An honoured place. Within the hearts of men
I heard the echo of my own creation,
And I was happy, taking calm delight
In labour and success, and hope of fame.
Happy, moreover, when my friends and comrades,
Fellows, not rivals, in the noble service,
Had their reward. Never, I swear it, never
Did jealousy or envy stir in me,
Never! not even when Piccini's art
Enraptured Paris—nor when, for the first time,
I heard the opening chords of Iphigenia.
Who can accuse me, who has known Salieri
At any time show pride, contempt or envy,
Or like an injured snake, in impotent fury,
Biting the earth? Yet now—'tis I that say it—
Now I am jealous, deep and agonising
My jealousy. Oh God, how can it be,
Where is the justice, when the sacred gift,
When the immortal genius is bestowed
Not on a self-denying passionate love,
On toil and discipline, on prayer and fasting,
But glows about the head of an imbecile,
An idle frivoller? O Mozart, Mozart—

Being a genius, Mozart is devoid of doubt and
envy. His creative activity seems to be effortless,
and he delights in it like a child. Like a child,
too, he is forgetful of himself and generous to
others. The mediocre Salieri, on the other hand,
who wavers in his belief in himself, especially in
the presence of such a wonder as Mozart, is full
of rancour and cruel egoism. Yet he is presented

by Pushkin as a Hamlet-like character, and his tortuous complexity comes out during his conversation with the transparently simple Mozart. Salieri hates through admiration, and admires through hatred. While listening to the "frivoller's" music, he realises more than ever before that its perfection is like God's Grace—something which cannot be imitated; and that Mozart is, quite *undeservedly*, in a different category from Salieri himself and hundreds of other hard-working musicians. Who would ever want to listen to *their* music on hearing the melodies of Mozart? Or who would still dare to write music at all? There certainly is "no justice in heaven above." But if so, Salieri wants to see justice done at least on earth—by killing Mozart. In his opinion, the death of Mozart is necessary for the sake of music itself; or for the sake of the musicians who are crushed and paralysed by his genius. Once Mozart is gone, even he, Salieri, may perhaps find enough courage to create again. In his sophisticated reasoning he wants to kill Mozart in order to save music. Actually, however, he is anxious through Mozart's death to reduce music itself to his own level and keep it there. He himself is certainly not a genius, and knows it, especially when Mozart is present. But could he not become one, if he got rid of Mozart through poison and thus restored his own self-confidence? Still, why should a crime be necessary in order to make him believe in himself? His Hamlet-like

mind is astir with the problem, and at the mention
of the possible crime on the part of Beaumarchais
(who was suspected of having poisoned his two
wives) Salieri himself hastens to answer:

> I don't believe it. He was too jolly a man
> For such a trade.

Quite unaware of what is going on in Salieri's
mind, Mozart completes his remark by saying:

> He was a genius
> Like you and me, and genius and crime
> Are incompatible things. Isn't it true?

"That's your opinion," replies Salieri, and
secretly drops poison in Mozart's glass. But when
Mozart drinks he suddenly wants to stop him,
as though still uncertain whether to commit the
crime or not. Another striking feature of the
situation is that Mozart has unconscious fore-
bodings of what is in store for him. Having
unwittingly drunk the poison, he plays on the
piano his own *Requiem,* and with such feeling that
tears come into Salieri's eyes.

MOZART: But why do you weep?
SALIERI: These tears
Are the first I ever shed, a pain, a pleasure,
As if I had paid off a heavy debt.
As if the surgeon's knife had cut away
An agonising limb. Forget my tears.
Play on and drench my soul in melody.
MOZART: I would that all could feel the power of
    music

As you, Salieri! No, for then the world
Would fade and perish. None would give a
     thought
To life's necessities. But you and I
Are of the chosen few, the priests of art,
Despisers of a coarse utility
And worshippers of Beauty. Isn't it true?
But I am unwell; I must lie down and sleep.
Goodbye.
SALIERI: Good night. (*Mozart goes out.*)
You will sleep long, my friend.
If he is right, I am no genius.
What did he say?—that genius and crime
Are incompatible things. I don't believe it.
What about Michelangelo?[1]
                      Or is it
The gossip of the brainless herd—a fable?

It was no murderer built the Vatican.

So this "little tragedy" ends on a note of Hamlet-
like doubt. No problems have been solved by it.
But they have been powerfully stated, or at least
suggested. And this is what art is for.

III

Equally simple and yet complicated is *The
Miser Knight*. This time the theme is avarice, but
Pushkin treats it neither in the spirit of Molière's

[1] This line refers to the once current rumour that Michelangelo had crucified his model in order to obtain a clearer idea
of what Christ (whom he was painting) must have looked like
on the cross. Pushkin may have obtained this *motif* from
several sources, and above all from Karamzin's *Letters of a Russian
Traveller* (XXII).

L'Avare nor of Shakespeare's *The Merchant of Venice*. It is questionable whether Pushkin had read *Aularia* by Plautus, but he knew *The Merchant of Venice*, *L'Avare*, possibly Ben Jonson's *Volpone* and Goldoni's *Il vero amico* (*The True Friend*) in which the miser's monologue reminds one of Pushkin's own knight. Avarice is also the theme of Milman's tragedy, *Fazio*, printed in the Galignani volume. At the first glance it may seem that Pushkin had divided Shylock into his meaner and what might be called "loftier" halves, the first being represented by the Jewish money-lender and the second by the knight. But he modified the problem of avarice considerably, and made the miser himself rather romantic. Whereas Harpagon and Shylock belong to the bourgeois class, Pushkin's miser is a feudal knight, that is, a man socially as remote from the acquisitive class as possible, although the on-coming power of money, with its new scale of values, is suggested by the theme itself. Yet Pushkin's knight is a miser not for the sake of money but for the sake of an idea. His moving spirit is the consciousness of power—through the possession of immense wealth. Contemptuous of the world and its enjoyments, he derives a kind of ecstatic pleasure from the knowledge that, however unassuming his appearance, he yet wields a potential might transcending the dreams of any mortal. The Russian literary historian Alexis Veselovsky thinks that such a character

may have been suggested to Pushkin by the
miser in Byron's *Don Juan* (Canto XII):

> While he, despising every sensual call,
> Commands—the intellectual lord of all.

Pushkin's miser, too, knows that any command
or whim of his could be gratified at a moment's
notice, and says so unashamedly in his famous
soliloquy (scene II) in the cellar, amidst his
coffers full of gold:

Like a young rake waiting to keep his tryst
With some sly wanton harlot of the town,
Or a poor fool seduced by him. So I
All day wait for the moment to descend
To my close vault to see my trusty coffers.
O blessed day! For on it I can pour
In the sixth chest (the chest as yet unfilled)
A handful of the heaped and shining gold.
Little enough it seems, but, though it is little,
The treasure grows and grows. I've read some-
    where
That once a king gave orders to his soldiers
To carry soil by handfuls to a heap,
And thus a proud hill grew from which the king
Could from a height look down, and see with joy
The valley dotted over with white tents,
The sea with ships gliding across its breast.
So I too—by poor handfuls patiently
Here to my cellar bring my wonted tribute,
And so I build my hill, and from its height
I can look down on all that owns my sway.
What does not own my sway? I, like some demon,
From here can dominate the universe.

I have but to wish. Palaces rise straightway,
And through the thickets of my glorious gardens
Fair nymphs go running in a merry crowd.
The Muses bring their tribute to my feet.
Free Genius is my slave and works for me,
Virtue and Toil labouring sleeplessly
Will humbly wait on me for recompense.
I shall but whistle and submissively
Will bloodstained Crime come crawling to my
    feet,
Timidly lick my hand, look in my eyes,
And read in them the signal of my will.
All shall be subject to me, I to nothing.
Out-stripping all desires I shall know peace;
I understand my power; this knowledge
Will be enough for me.

Yet it all proves to be a delusion. In reality
he does not and cannot command. It is herein
that his tragedy consists, aggravated by the conflict with his own spendthrift son. This conflict,
analogous to the one between Harpagon and
Cléante in Molière's L'Avare, is psychologically
complicated by the son's unconscious or half-
conscious wish for his father's death. Strangely
enough, the animosity between father and son
is not devoid of a disguised autobiographical
character. Pushkin's father too (like the Miser
Knight) kept his own son in penury—especially
during the poet's first Petersburg period. A
well-known Pushkinist (V. Khodasevich) even
points out that the Miser's accusation of his
rebellious son in scene III is similar to Pushkin's

father's false accusation that his son had laid hands on him, as described in the letter to Zhukovsky from Mikhaylovskoye on October 31st, 1824. In the play itself the Knight's will to power is shown as being sterile because it does not spring from a wish to expand or intensify life. So it warps and frustrates even those lives which are potentially broad and intense. Instead of the world of realities, it only chooses the dark stuffy cellars, where the Miser gloats over his ducats all the more greedily because they represent concentrated human suffering. His formula ("I understand my power; this knowledge will be enough for me") degrades him to a perverted ascetic and eventually leads to destruction and self-destruction. Having sacrificed his life to his own will to power, he loses both. Instead of being master of his wealth he becomes its slave and victim. *The Miser Knight* was to have been first performed on February 1st, 1837, but owing to Pushkin's death had to be cancelled.

IV

The title of Pushkin's last and formally most perfect "little tragedy," *The Stone Guest*, was taken from Tirso de Molina's play on the same subject, *El burlador de Sevilla y convidado de piedra*. It consists of four scenes only, but these make an admirable masterpiece on a theme which, before Pushkin, had intrigued many authors: from Tirso de

Molina to Molière and Goldoni; from Da Ponte (Mozart's librettist) to E. T. A. Hoffmann, and from Byron to Musset, Balzac, Stendhal and Lenau. Its history was old and chequered. Tirso de Molina's play was performed, in Molière's time, by an Italian troupe in Paris. Molière took up the theme and worked it out, not in verse but in prose—probably in order to make it appeal to wider audiences. A Russian translation of Molière's *Le Festin de pierre* was produced in Petersburg in 1816, and its performances continued. A ballet on the same subject was very popular during the 'twenties both in Petersburg and Moscow. So was Mozart's *Don Giovanni*. There was of course a variety of interpretations of the theme itself in European literature— whether dramatic or otherwise. Tirso de Molina and Molière even seem to have treated it as a warning example of the "vicious" feudal class. Others stressed that epicurean attitude which discarded, and with good conscience, the medieval fear of the flesh: Da Ponte, for example. Byron's *Don Juan* was a satirical attack on the ruling society of his day. Hoffmann, Musset and Lenau were more concerned, however, with man's eternal quest for the ideal woman through a series of disappointments in actual women.

Pushkin's own approach combines the Mozart-Da Ponte attitude with a hidden cult of love for its own sake. His Don Juan is an epicurean and an adroit gallant (the episode with Laura), brimming over with the exuberance of life—Pushkin's own counterpart as it were. It is Don Juan's thirst for intense life that drives him from one woman to another, and the paradox of it is that the very sincerity of his quest makes him inconstant. He is in love with love rather than with women. Yet underneath his carnal adventures there smoulders an unconscious craving for the perfect woman, and this desire flares up in his contact with the dead commander's wife, Doña Anna. In Pushkin's play the commander had been killed by Don Juan in a conflict before the latter knew Doña Anna at all. He meets her for the first time at her husband's tomb and falls in love. When after much hesitation Doña Anna invites him to her house, he with joking recklessness bids the statue of her dead husband to come too and stand guard outside her door. But once in her house, Don Juan no longer hides his identity from Doña Anna, whose strange feminine charm seems to cast a hitherto unknown spell over him. She is frightened, but he tries to allay her fears by this confession about himself:

He [Don Juan] was, I have no doubt, described to you
As scoundrel, rogue and traitor, Doña Anna.
Maybe the rumour was not all untrue.
Upon my burdened conscience many crimes
Weigh heavily, perhaps, for in the school
Of vice for long I've been an eager pupil.
But from the time when first I saw your face

It seemed to me that I was born again.
For, loving you, I feel in love with virtue,
And for the first time in humility
Before her down I fall on trembling knees.

DOÑA ANNA: O yes, Don Juan's eloquent I know:
I've heard that he's a very skilful artist.
You arrant fiend, how many helpless women
Have you destroyed?

DON JUAN: And not a single one
Among them have I loved!

DOÑA ANNA: I'm to believe
Don Juan's fall'n in love for the first time
And that I am not just his latest victim?

DON JUAN: If I indeed were trying to entrap you,
Would I confess and speak that name to you,
The very sound of which you can't endure.
What's here of guile and evil machination?

But at the moment when, under the spell of
Anna's beauty, Don Juan is on the threshold of a
new life, the heavy steps of the commander's
statue (a symbol of Juan's guilty conscience) are
heard at the door. Don Juan's first profound
and transforming love is thus not allowed to
mature. His own past blocks the way for him and
hurls him to destruction. It is not too much to
say that Pushkin, who in his youth had been
something of an indefatigable Don Juan (even
possessing a list of the women who had loved
him), must have felt a similar change in the

presence of his beautiful fiancée, to whom he addressed the sonnet *Madonna*. But, like Don Juan, he too must have felt the weight of his former dissipations. Together with the sonnet *Madonna*, his poem *Memory* can perhaps provide a key to the inner meaning of *The Stone Guest*, reflecting as it were the poet's own moral dilemma, roughly from 1826 onwards, when he first began to think of marriage.

Reading the past with horror, shame and dread,
I tremble and I curse,
But the repentant tears, the bitter tears I shed,
Will not wash out a single verse.

As was pointed out already in 1841 by Pushkin's friend and critic S. Shevyryov, certain passages of the scene between Don Juan and Doña Anna are reminiscent of Gloucester's address to Lady Anne ("If thy revengeful heart cannot forgive") in *Richard III*. And Doña Anna's complaint about the loss of her husband, which makes her mix, "like April," tears with smiles is similar to that of another widow (Isabella) in Barry Cornwall's little play, *Ludovico Sforza*, scene II:

              Even I, you see,
Although a widow, not divested of
Her sorrows quite, am here i' the midst of tears
To smile, like April, on you.

V

The Stone Guest was published posthumously in 1839 and performed in Petersburg in 1847. Incidentally, this was Pushkin's first play to be presented to foreign audiences. Translated by Turgenev and Viardot, it was produced at the theatre Port Saint Martin in Paris in February 1877, and had great success. Another play by Pushkin published after his death was his unfinished The Water Fairy (Rusalka), which may be classed as one of his miniature plays, although it is considerably longer than any of the four "little tragedies." Having started it in 1829, Pushkin resumed it again in 1832, perhaps under the influence of the now forgotten but in those days popular opera Das Donauweibchen (The Danube Maid), a "romantic-comical folk-tale" by K. F. Hensler.[1] Pushkin's first editor, Annenkov, would have it that the Water Fairy was planned as a kind of libretto for an opera, presumably to be written by the composer A. Petrov-Esaulov, with South-Russian folklore and folk-music as one of its ingredients.

[1] Pushkin refers to a melody from Donauweibchen in his Evgeny Onegin (chapter II, 12):

> He enters—and the talk shifts duly
> Aside, upon the weary life
> That a man lives without a wife.
> Then to the tea-urn in the middle
> They call him. Dunya, pouring, hears
> The whisper, "Notice!" in her ears;
> The next she fetches out her fiddle,
> And—O, good Lord! is squealing now:
> "Come to my golden chamber, thou!"

The plot is simple. A young prince falls in love with a miller's daughter, whom he seduces and then abandons in order to marry a woman of his own rank. The girl drowns herself in the Dnieper, and becomes a water-fairy. Her daughter, born at the bottom of the river, is also a *rusalka*.[1] The old miller, who had once cunningly encouraged his daughter's flirtation with the prince, goes mad with grief. His watermill falls into ruin. But the prince finds no happiness in his marriage. Sad and restless, he is impelled to revisit the haunts of his former love. During one such walk he encounters on the bank of the Dnieper an entrancing young maiden: the fairy daughter of his betrayed sweetheart, obviously sent to entice him into the river as a punishment for his crime. The concluding scene has either been lost or else was left unwritten. But even without it, *The Water Fairy* is a poetically perfect thing.

Different in every way is his dramatic fragment in prose, *Scenes from Feudal Times*, dating from the middle of the 'thirties and slightly reminiscent of Mérimée's *La Jacquerie* (1828). Pushkin apparently intended to write a drama on a big scale about the conflict between feudalism and the ascendant bourgeoisie. The social background was to be the disintegration of the feudal age, a

---

[1] An identical *motif* is to be found in *Prince Yanysh* among Pushkin's sixteen *Songs of Western Slavs*, eleven of which he translated from Mérimée's *La Guzla*. *Prince Yanysh* was turned into a fine ballad also by the Polish poet Mickiewicz.

process which was partly connected with the invention of gun-powder and book-printing. Judging by the scenes left, the play would have been a highly concentrated drama of realistic mass movement—like Schiller's *Wilhelm Tell* or, more recently, Hauptmann's *Weavers*—based on a problem which had its analogy in Pushkin's Russia, preparing to liquidate her own feudal era. Another big theme, connected with Western feudalism in its dark period, was to deal with the supposed woman pope Joanna (ninth century). The *motif* itself may have been suggested to Pushkin by the Italian poet B. B. Casti, who had made use of it in his poem, *La Popessa*, or perhaps by the contents of a German fifteenth-century mystery play about the woman-pope Yutta, an account of which was found, after his death, in a book he had in his library. Pushkin seems to have wavered whether to work it out in the form of a play or of a narrative poem "in the style of *Christabel*" by Coleridge, but all that he left was a brief sketch (in French) for the play.

It may seem a pity that Pushkin did not exploit his dramatic vein to the end. But after 1831 he became increasingly interested in prose, and his achievements in this direction were so important that they can be regarded as one of the foundations of modern Russian prose in general. It is this section of Pushkin's work that still remains to be examined.

Chapter Nine

Pushkin's Works in Prose

I

OWING to his strong realistic sense Pushkin was bound to adopt, sooner or later, prose too as a suitable medium for depicting Russian life. Besides, in the third chapter of *Evgeny Onegin* he himself promised to do so:

> And now, perhaps, by heaven's decree
> I shall no longer be a poet;
> Some other fiend will enter me.
> I will scorn Phoebus' frowns, and wholly
> Descend to prose, however lowly;
> Then some old-fashioned tale shall still
> Engross, and cheer, my path downhill.
> Not there shall grimly be invented
> A villain's secret pangs of soul,
> But just a Russian house's whole
> Annals shall simply be presented,
> With love's alluring visions, and
> The antique manners of the land.

Pushkin kept his promise. Not that his poetic genius was getting tired or exhausted. One of the reasons was his desire to explore the possibilities of prose in the same way as he had explored the possibilities of verse. Here too he proved to be a pioneer, and was largely responsible for the character of modern Russian prose, which he imbued with the same "naked beauty" as his poems. He himself insisted that "precision and brevity are the primary virtues of prose. They demand thoughts and more thoughts, which brilliant expressions cannot replace." It was "brilliant expressions" that he avoided most of all.

The state of Russian prose in the 'twenties and 'thirties was far from satisfactory. The "precious" style of Karamzin's tales belonged to another age. So did the rhetorical manner which he used in his *History*. V. Narezhny's narratives suffered from crudeness of style and composition. The didactic-adventurous novel *Ivan Vyzhigin* (1829) by the notorious *canaille littéraire* T. Bulgarin, although a "best seller" at the time, was a belated and not very palatable Russian offspring of *Gil Blas*. M. Zagoskin, the first important Russian follower of Sir Walter Scott, was more enjoyable as a narrator than as an artist. One of the highly popular authors, A. Bestuzhev-Marlinsky, adopted the "furious" romantic style (with a sprinkling of *Ossian* and Sterne) which came from France, whereas A. Veltman and Prince V. Odoevsky bore evident traces of German romanticism.[1] In Russia prose was as yet too

---

[1] Bestuzhev-Marlinsky wrote, amongst other things, several historical narratives evidently influenced by Sir Walter Scott, whose popularity in Russia was at its height between 1820 and 1830, that is, after the vogue of Richardson, Sterne, Goldsmith and Mrs. Radcliffe.

little differentiated from poetry to be really good. Excellent prose was written, however, by the poet P. Vyazemsky; and in the years when Pushkin began printing his own stories and narratives another master of Russian prose, Nikolai Gogol (1809–52), was making his début, but in a direction which was different from that of Pushkin and made a number of concessions to Gogol's own romantic temperament.

In contrast to Gogol's ornate and exuberant style, Pushkin adopted from the outset a deliberate matter-of-fact conciseness, which he raised to the highest artistic level. Although primarily a poet, he would never confuse the methods of poetry with those of prose. Using the latter as a medium entitled to its own laws, he emancipated it from all "poetic" propensities in the name of an intimate and homely realism. And if he was not the first to introduce the "little man" into Russian fiction (Karamzin had forestalled him in this), he yet democratised and at the same time vitalised Russian literary language by including in it a number of idioms and inflections taken from the people's speech. In this manner he not only raised the level of Russian prose but also enlarged its basis.

II

Pushkin's début in prose was connected, significantly enough, with his favourite hero,

Peter I. Such works as *Boris Godunov, Poltava* and *The Bronze Horseman* prove that his interest in Russia's past never flagged. And so, having switched over from verse to prose, he first thought of an historical novel—a *genre* which Scott had made popular in those days all over Europe. *The Negro of Peter the Great*, begun in 1827, never went beyond the first six chapters and a small portion of the seventh. Yet even as it is, it represents a splendid attempt at writing an historical narrative modelled on the pattern provided by Scott but worked out according to Pushkin's own realistic method and the principle of "naked beauty." Apart from giving us a portrait of Peter the Great in his more ordinary human aspects, Pushkin also shows us eighteenth-century manners, especially those of Petersburg, in their authentic light. But since the central hero of the novel was to be his own maternal ancestor Ibrahim Hannibal, the novel obviously aimed at becoming a "Russian house's annals" against the background of the Europeanisation of Russia. This makes one doubly regret that it remained unfinished.

Among Pushkin's works in prose the modest book *Tales of Belkin* (1830) comes next. The five stories it contains—intensified and stripped to their anecdotic essentials—are now commonly regarded as masterpieces, although they aroused little attention when first published: their art was too much of the kind that conceals art. Like Scott in his *Tales of My Landlord*, Pushkin, too, here ingeniously put between himself and the reader a supposed narrator, Belkin, whose personal tone and inflection are preserved. Belkin takes the reader in turns to the Russian country house, the post-coach station, the suburban artisans' quarter and to army circles, often evincing that sense of humour which is the more effective by being or rather by appearing unconscious. Pushkin was thus able to exercise his own humour or parody in an indirect manner. One of the stories, *The Post-Stage Master*, for example, is a mild parody of Karamzin's best-known sentimental narrative *Poor Liza* (depicting the tragedy of a lower-class girl who loved a nobleman), as well as of the biblical parable of the prodigal son. Unlike Karamzin, Pushkin gives his romance a happy ending. Quite in contrast to the prodigal son, the "prodigal" daughter, who had eloped from her aged father's house with a handsome aristocrat, was happy ever after. It was not she who came to grief, but her father, with his biblical outlook and attitude. *The Snowstorm* is supposed to parody another sentimental story (*Natalia*) by Karamzin. *The Undertaker*, with its lower-class characters, pokes fun at the romantic ghost stories much in vogue at the time. Love between a nobleman and a pretended village-girl is the theme of *The Peasant-Lady*, permeated with the atmosphere of the Russian countryside. Even when tackling such a romantic motive—the postponement of vengeance—as the one developed

in *The Shot*, Pushkin makes the somewhat un-
common subject-matter convincing by the naturalness of his style and tone.

Linked with these stories is Pushkin's unfinished
satire on the serf-system, *A History of the Village
Goryukhino*, since once again the supposed narrator
(or in this case the compiler) is Belkin. Both
works were written at the same time: during the
prolific autumn weeks at Boldino in 1830. The
mixture of *naïveté* and "unconscious" satire with
which Belkin unfolds the annals of a village
victimised by the brutality of the system only
strengthens the final effect. But aware of the dead
hand of the censorship, Pushkin discontinued this
promising "history." [1] He presented, however,
some further aspects of serfdom in *Dubrovsky*
(1832–3). The hero of this novel is decidedly
romantic: a polished young nobleman, turned
brigand in order to take revenge upon the all-
powerful magnate who ruined his father. The
tradition of the idealized or noble brigand, from
Schiller's Karl Moor (*The Robbers*) to *Jean Sbogar*
by Charles Nodier, was still strong at the time,
not to mention Pushkin's old interest in the Volga
bandits. The serfs joining their ruined young
master as rebels against the self-willed feudal
magnate suggest, at least potentially, a social

---

[1] It is supposed to parody the *History of Russian People* by Polevoy,
a critic whose romantic sympathies were antagonistic to the
views of Nadezhdin. In a recent study of Pushkin (by M.
Alekseyev, Odessa 1927) a certain similarity between *Goryukhino*
and Washington Irving's *A History of New York* is pointed out.

strain in Pushkin's novel, although the romance as such preponderates. Pushkin makes the magnate's daughter fall in love with the charming brigand who, disguised as a French tutor, lives in her father's house. Such a disguise gave Pushkin a pretext for a realistic picture of the rough provincial gentry under Catherine II. Corrupt officialdom, with its practice of bribery and intimidation, also received its due.

Another example of a romantic theme handled with even greater realistic terseness is *The Queen of Spades* (1834), a story which makes one think of Hoffmann, but rewritten in the lucid, compact prose of Voltaire, Stendhal or Mérimée. Pushkin describes in it the tragedy of a certain Herrmann —a thrifty Russified German who frightened a decrepit countess to death by trying to obtain from her the secret of winning a fortune at cards. After her burial the countess appears to Herrmann at night and reveals to him the coveted secret. He at first wins a huge sum of money, then stakes the whole of it and loses. The shock makes him go mad. This Petersburgian *novella* is, apart from *The Gipsies*, the most condensed work Pushkin ever wrote. If there is such a thing as dynamic dryness, we find it here. Yet both the story and its background—the atmosphere of the 'twenties, —are for this very reason all the more effective.

III

History of the Pugachov Rebellion (1833–4) and
A Captain's Daughter (1836) should be examined
together. Both resulted from Pushkin's interest
in the rebellion against Catherine II in 1773
under the leadership of the illiterate Emelyan
Pugachov, who, posing as the fugitive Peter III
(Catherine's "liquidated" husband), fomented a
revolt among the Ural Cossacks, as well as among
the serfs on the Lower Volga. Having been allowed
to work, from 1833 onwards, in the State Archives,
Pushkin had access to all sorts of documents connected with the rising. He also undertook a
journey to the regions concerned. The first result
of all this was to be a history of Pugachov himself. After Nicholas I had objected to it on the
ground that a rebel like Pugachov "has no
history," Pushkin altered the title, but even
so he concentrated mainly on Pugachov and
was wise enough to abstain (for reasons
of censorship) from delving deeper into the
social causes of the rebellion, though he was
perfectly aware of them. This laconic—almost
too laconic—historical work can hardly be
dissociated from Pushkin's historical novel, *A
Captain's Daughter*, which he started in 1833
and completed only in 1836. As in the case of
The Negro of Peter the Great, here too the Waverley
Novels may have exercised a certain influence,
yet without infringing upon Pushkin's own

originality.[1] Its length is about one-third of a novel by Scott, and its disciplined style and language are uniformly superb.

A Captain's Daughter is told in the first person by the chief character, Grinyov—a young nobleman, almost à boy, who shortly before the events of 1773 was sent by his father to do military service in a God-forsaken little fortress near the Urals. On the way, he and his old servant Savelyich were caught by a blizzard. During the blizzard Grinyov gave a lift to a strayed wanderer and with the impulsive generosity of a boy presented him with a fur coat. This chance meeting linked in a strange manner Grinyov's fate with that of Pugachov. For the wanderer whose life he had thus saved was none other than the subsequent leader of the rebellious Cossacks. Once in the fortress, Grinyov developed a profound attachment for Masha, the daughter of his chief, Captain Mironov—a simple, honest soul bossed by his equally simple and honest wife. The rising started. It soon spread like wildfire, piling horror upon horror: murder, plunder, vengeance and cruelty for its own sake. Grinyov was compelled to hide Masha from his unscrupulous rival Shvabrin (who subsequently joined the rebels) and also from Pugachov himself, whose interest in the fair sex was notorious. The little fort was taken. Its inhabitants were terrorised into sub-

---

[1] Two of Scott's novels which may here be taken into account are *The Heart of Midlothian* and *The Bride of Lammermoor*.

mission. Mironov died loyal to his duty, while his wife died loyal to him. This is what happened in the market-place of the fallen fortress, as described by Grinyov:

"Pugachov was sitting in an arm-chair on the steps of the Commandant's house. He was wearing a red Cossack coat trimmed with gold braid. A tall sable cap with golden tassels was pushed low over his glittering eyes. His face seemed familiar to me. The Cossack elders surrounded him. Father Gerasim [the priest], pale and trembling, was standing by the steps with a cross in his hands, and seemed to be silently imploring mercy for the future victims. Gallows were being hastily put up in the market-place. As we approached, the Bashkirs dispersed the crowd and brought us before Pugachov. The bells stopped ringing; there was a profound stillness.

" 'Which is the Commandant?' the Pretender asked.

"Our Cossack sergeant stepped out of the crowd and pointed to Ivan Kuzmich [Mironov]. Pugachov looked at the old man menacingly and said to him:

" 'How did you dare resist me, your Tsar?' "

"Exhausted by his wound, the Commandant mustered his last strength and answered in a firm voice:

" 'You are not my Tsar; you are a thief and a pretender, let me tell you.'

"Pugachov frowned darkly and waved a white

handkerchief. Several Cossacks seized the old Captain and dragged him to the gallows. The old Bashkir whom he had questioned the night before was sitting astride the cross-beam. He was holding a rope, and a minute later I saw poor Ivan Kuzmich swinging in the air."

It would be impossible to depict so gruesome a scene in a more detached manner. We also learn that Grinyov himself escaped Mironov's fate only because Pugachov suddenly recognised in him his one-time benefactor. From then on Grinyov, whom the rebel leader treated as a guest rather than a prisoner, was able to follow the horrors of the *jacquerie* in the entire region, until the professional armies sent to quench it proved too much for the rebels. Pugachov was caught and later publicly executed in Moscow. Grinyov was at first under the suspicion of having been one of Pugachov's adherents, but after his rescued fiancée's journey to Petersburg and her interview with the Empress Catherine II, all ended well. The happiness of the two lovers was no longer disturbed by any calamities, personal or otherwise.

It is worth noting that Pushkin visited Pugachov's former headquarters, the village of Berda near Orenburg, where he obtained some valuable information from an old woman eye-witness. His own attitude towards the revolt was negative, since he looked upon it from the angle of an enlightened nobleman and a hater of violence.

This did not prevent him from doing justice to Pugachov, whom he portrayed not as a villain pure and simple but as a puzzling mixture of extremes, devoid of anything half-hearted or lukewarm. He could be exceedingly cruel, but never mean. Nor was there any calculation in his occasional generosity. Fundamentally, his was a "broad" Russian nature, full of vitality and with tremendous possibilities for both good and evil.

The narrator, Grinyov, is youthfully frank and impulsive, with an instinctive sense of what is right. His groom Savelyich represents the old patriarchal house-serf. A member of the family rather than a slave, he is always grumbling but at the same time fanatically devoted: father and mother in one to his young master. Such unsophisticated decent folk as the Mironovs, who accept their own positions in life without questioning, belong to the patriarchal group-mentality with its values of good and evil set once and for all. They would not think of swerving from them. Nor would their daughter Masha, who is submissive by nature but brave and firm when necessary. Grinyov's rival Shvabrin conforms to the traditional villain-type; it is quite possible that, while shaping him, Pushkin had in mind the type of a *déclassé* from the gentry who joined the lower strata only from base opportunist motives. Be this as it may, he fits into the pattern of the novel, in which not only the characters but also history and manners are perfectly adjusted.

IV

Among Pushkin's minor works and fragments *A Romance in Letters* (1829–30) is of particular interest to English readers. It is done in the epistolary form as created by Richardson, to whose *Clarissa Harlowe* Pushkin refers. In it he tackles the social problem to which he attached great importance at the time: the historical rôle, the tasks and prospects of his own class. The two more or less finished works of that period are the short story *Kirdjali* (1834) and his *Journey to Erzerum* (1829, printed in 1836). *Roslavlev*, *A Russian Pelham*, and the prose part of *The Egyptian Nights* (which looks like the beginning of a novel of manners) remained fragments.

The anecdotic story *Kirdjali* recalls to one's mind Pushkin's Bessarabian days, Ypsilanti's Greek insurgents, and his own interest in the reckless brigand-type. Its hero is a Bulgarian bandit who had joined Ypsilanti and then escaped to Kishinev, where he was caught and delivered to the Turks. While waiting for execution at Jassy, he tricked his guards, escaped once more, and began to terrorise the whole of the district. A *Journey to Erzerum* is a record of the poet's journey in the Caucasus in 1829, when he visited the Russian army near the Turkish fortress of Erzerum and the captured Erzerum itself—the only place outside Russia he had ever seen. As for *Roslavlev*, its very title is identical with one of Zagoskin's novels (written in the manner of Sir Walter Scott) about Russia during Napoleon's invasion in 1812. But unlike Zagoskin he intended to give an objective realistic picture of that period as seen through the eyes of a woman. While drawing on the observations of Mme de Staël,[1] whose stay in Russia coincided with Napoleon's invasion, Pushkin chose for his heroine his one-time love— the intelligent and intensely patriotic Princess Avdotya Golitsina.

A Russian Pelham, of which only the plan is known, reminds one again of English literature: this time of the well-known but hardly outstanding novel by Bulwer Lytton. The title does not necessarily mean that Pushkin was anxious to imitate the English novelist. What he wanted to do was to write a novel of adventure, as if designed to counteract Bulgarin's vulgar *Ivan Vyzhigin* in the same way as *Roslavlev* was meant to counteract Zagoskin. As far as one can gauge, Pushkin's work was to have been also a social novel of manners, perhaps with his Moscow friend Nashchokin as a Russian Pelham. Nashchokin was a typical Moscow character of those days. A millionaire, a bohemian, a gambler and a spendthrift, he alternately won and lost several fortunes. But in spite of his extravagant habits he was yet a sensitive man, endowed with artistic

[1] Recorded in her book, *Dix années d'exil*. Pushkin was an admirer of Mme de Staël, whose championship of national literatures (quite in the romantic spirit) appealed to him very much.

taste and appreciation. Pushkin valued his friendship, and often stayed with him while in Moscow. One can well imagine what he would have made of such a model had he gone beyond the few initial jottings for the novel.

Finally, a place of honour in Russian prose is allotted to Pushkin's critical notes, articles, and most particularly his letters. In criticism he showed a literary knowledge which was no less astonishing than his discrimination. His judgments, while always to the point, are full of wit and of that almost clairvoyant common sense which was an inalienable feature of his intelligence. The same applies to his letters, the bubbling humour and spontaneity of which are unsurpassed in Russian literature.

Chapter Ten

Pushkin's Place in Literature

I

"PUSHKIN is one of the phenomena that live and move eternally," wrote the critic Belinsky after the poet's death. "His existence continues in the consciousness of his readers. Each epoch, regardless of the rightness of its understanding, passes its own judgment on him, and at the same time leaves it to the next epoch to add something, without ever exhausting the whole truth about him."

This verdict gains in weight if we take into consideration the time in which Pushkin lived and worked. It was a time when the romantic movement had put an end to the dictatorship of French pseudo-classicism all over Europe and stressed the importance of national spirit and peculiarities in literature. Pushkin concluded the period which began with Lomonosov and culminated in Derzhavin. At the same time he determined the character of Russian national literature by providing it with that broad outlook and perspective which saved it from the danger of provinciality, as well as from any sort of nationalistic smugness. In his hands Russian literature became more European than ever, but on a truly Russian basis.

It is also important to realise that his death coincided with a moment when the whole of Russian culture was at the crossroads, i.e. passing from the gentry-period (the culmination of which was Pushkin) to that intelligentsia-period which lasted until the recent revolution. The members of the intelligentsia, with Belinsky as their recognised leader, followed with certain misgivings the last phase of Pushkin's life, perhaps without knowing enough about the fatal circumstances behind it. But once he was dead they were the first to recognise the greatness of his genius. What mattered to them was no longer Pushkin the "courtier" but Pushkin the poet and the martyr of a system which he himself had loathed all along. True enough, after the Crimean War, when the intelligentsia came into their own, the ultra-radical critic Pisarev made his notorious onslaught on Pushkin's æsthetic trend, which he proclaimed as useless or even harmful in the welter of sober utilitarian aims and activities so typical of the 'sixties. But another leader of the radical intelligentsia, Chernyshevsky, who was much less of a sectarian, not only defended Pushkin the poet but laid emphasis on the fact that through him literature itself had become a powerful social force in Russia. "It was through Pushkin," he wrote, "that literary culture penetrated to thousands of men, whereas before him only a handful of people took any interest in it at all. He was the first among us to raise literature to a dignified function, vital for the whole of our nation, whereas before him it was—as a periodical aptly put it—but a pleasant and useful pastime for a narrow circle of dilettanti. He was the first poet to occupy in the eyes of the whole of Russia that high and incontestable position which, in each country, belongs but to a truly great poet."

Even this verdict, however just, does not by a long way exhaust the whole of Pushkin's significance. He not only completed the reform of the Russian literary language without breaking with a tradition which goes—via Karamzin—back to Lomonosov, but also filled the gap between the literature of his country and that of the world. He did this by organically incorporating in Russian literature the values and the methods of its more advanced Western sisters, while still remaining a Russian in the best sense of this word.

II

It is no exaggeration to say that in Pushkin's works the Russian literary language reached its perfection. It was above all the solemn "romantic phrase" that Pushkin strangled by his lucid classical realism, which he bequeathed—through Lermontov's novel *A Hero of our Time*—to Turgenev, Goncharov, Tolstoy and many others.

There was of course a parallel current, with its origin in the ornate and agitated style of Gogol, which was soon adopted by Dostoevsky and, more recently, by the symbolist Andrey Bely. On the other hand, Gogol himself owed a great deal to Pushkin, and frankly acknowledged it. Apart from obliterating the former distinction between the "high" and the "low" *genres*, Pushkin democratised the literary language itself by grafting upon it the idioms and the accent of the people.[1] As early as 1825 he was contending that the "speech of the simple folk must first be divorced from the literary language in order, later on, to unite with it, and thus provide the right medium for expressing our thoughts." Acting upon this principle, he anticipated those stylistic possibilities which subsequently found expression in the work of Nikolay Leskov and, in recent times, in that of Alexey Remizov, to which the writings of some Soviet authors could be added.

Another conspicuous fact is the persistence with which Pushkin's themes continued in Russian literature after him. It was not without significance that both romanticism and realism met in his works. If he was the first to feel the influence of Byron in Russia, he was also the first to overcome it. Yet after him the Russian Byronists continued to look for inspiration not so much to Byron himself as to the Pushkin of the Byronic

[1] A great deal in this respect was done also by Ivan Krylov (1768–1844), whose excellent fables are full of racy folk-speech and folk-idioms.

period. This is largely true even of the most Byronic of all the Russian poets, Michael Lermontov (1814–41). Lermontov, moreover, followed Pushkin in using the Caucasian (and also Crimean) background in his crisply written analytical novel *A Hero of our Time*. A. Bestuzhev-Marlinsky's gushing and once very popular narratives were to a large extent connected with the Caucasus.[1] The action of that delightful early novel by Leo Tolstoy *The Cossacks* (written in 1852, published in 1862) also takes place in a Caucasian setting, though the theme of the novel is a subtle parody of the fashion set up by *The Prisoner in the Caucasus*. Tolstoy's aristocratic Olenin, far from being a breaker of the Caucasian maidens' hearts, is himself spurned by the primitive Cossack-girl Marianka as being hardly worth while. Apart from several shorter sketches dealing with the Caucasus (including a splendid story for children under the same title as Pushkin's first Byronic tale in verse), Tolstoy returned to the Caucasian motives in *Hadji Murat*, one of his best posthumous novels.

Pushkin's realistic rather than romantic trend was endorsed by E. A. Baratynsky (1800–44) who, together with Vyazemsky, Yazykov and Delvig, formed the backbone of Pushkin's Pleiad. Baratynsky's three tales in verse, *Eda*, *The Ball* and *The Gipsy Girl*, were written, at least partially,

[1] He was a Decembrist, and was first sent to Siberia and later to the Caucasus. Like the Decembrist poets Ryleyev and Kyukhelbeker, he too was an ardent admirer of Byron.

under the influence of Pushkin. Of these, *Eda* is based on a theme resembling the one in *The Prisoner in the Caucasus* and in *The Gipsies*: the meeting of a civilised member of society with a "child of nature"—in this case a Finnish peasant-girl. The Caucasian background is replaced by the wild scenery of Finland, and Baratynsky's descriptions, too, are intensely realistic. The realistic humorous *genre* of Pushkin's *Little House in Kolomna* was taken up, with varying success, by Lermontov and several other poets (Ogaryov, Maykov, Polonsky, Fet and Alexis K. Tolstoy), whereas Nekrasov further developed Pushkin's poetry of indictment. *The Bronze Horseman* introduced the "little man" into narrative poetry, but it also stressed some of those haunting aspects of Petersburg which were later reflected by Apollon Grigoryev, N. Nekrasov and Alexander Blok in poetry, and by Gogol, Dostoevsky and, more recently, by Andrey Bely (in his novel *Petersburg*) in prose.

As for *Evgeny Onegin*, its influence upon poetry was smaller than upon the novel. Turgenev, who had started his career as a poet, must have been affected by it when writing his own narrative in verse, *Parasha* (1843). A. I. Polezhayev's (1805–38) *Sashka*, though of doubtful poetic value, was a flippant parody of *Onegin*, and that was all. Pushkin's "novel in verse" had to wait until the beginning of this century to find a worthy counterpart in the unfinished autobiography in verse *Retribution* (*Vozmézdie*) by Alexander Blok. The leader of Russian symbolism is also linked to the greatest of Russian classics by several other themes (including the dénouement of *The Stone Guest*) which he worked out in his own manner. Similarly, the early seditious poems of Pushkin found an echo not only in the "civic" verses of K. Ryleyev but in the revolutionary poetry of 1905 and that of 1917.

III

No less far-reaching was Pushkin's influence upon Russian prose. His *Tales of Belkin*, for instance, relegated Karamzin's stories to an irrevocable past as regards style and manner. But while enlarging the base of Russian literary language Pushkin also widened the social base of literature itself by introducing into it a great variety of characters: from Peter the Great and Catherine II to the unassuming Mironov and the humble "little man," all of whom he treated with the same care and the same artistic sympathy. Gogol's *Greatcoat* and Dostoevsky's *Poor Folk* came largely out of Pushkin's *Post-Stage Master*, and the rôle played by the first of these stories in the development of the "natural school" championed by Belinsky is known to every student of Russian literature. The strongest influence on Russian fiction—at least in its thematic aspects—was exercised, however, by *Evgeny Onegin*.

As has already been pointed out, Pushkin introduced his own equivalent of the Childe Harold type to Russian readers at a time when a number of ambitious but frustrated youths were a fact of Russian life. So this uprooted hero was soon adopted under the unromantic label of the "superfluous man," and gradually became the staple character of Russian realism. In Aleko we saw him being stripped of his romantic halo. In Onegin he was shown as a product of artificial Petersburg society and therefore hardly entitled to be more than a parody. He became tragic, however, in Lermontov's Pechorin, the chief character in the novel *A Hero of our Time.*[1] Pechorin is a further stage of the uprooted Onegin-type. He is an exceptionally strong and gifted individual, but frustrated by the atmosphere of the "leaden regime" which he is compelled to endure. So his own potential strength turns against itself and becomes destructive. His tragedy is that of the blind-alley, and through no fault of his own.

After Lermontov's Pechorin, the "superfluous man" began to invade Russian literature not as a fictitious but as a real product of Russian life. Beltov in Herzen's novel *Whose Fault* was a variety of the same character towards the end of the 'forties. Tentetnikov in the second part of Gogol's *Dead Souls* was another, and he led straight to the

[1] Another character of this novel, Maxim Maximych, is a literary descendant of Captain Mironov in Pushkin's *A Captain's Daughter.*

hero of Goncharov's masterpiece *Oblomov*. Turgenev who, incidentally, brought to perfection
Pushkin's method (so conspicuous in *Onegin*) of
rendering characters by means of a suggestive
lyrical "atmosphere" rather than through analysis, called one of his own narratives *The Diary of
a Superfluous Man*. The hero of his short novel
Rudin is equally "superfluous." So are Lavretsky
in *A Nest of Gentlefolk*, Litvinov in *Smoke* and the
Hamlet-like revolutionary Nezhdanov in *Virgin Soil*.
Chekhov—another great master of "atmosphere"
—actually specialised in "superfluous men,"
whose descendant crops up again in Gorky's
Foma Gordeyev, and even in *Cities and Years*, one
of the best early Soviet novels, by K. Fedin.

In Dostoevsky's works the "superfluous man"
became the "underworld man" who, in his social
and spiritual uprootedness, analysed away not
only his own self but the whole of existence, like
Raskolnikov in *Crime and Punishment*, Stavrogin in
The Possessed and Ivan in *The Brothers Karamazov*.
Pushkin's *Post-Stage Master*, on the other hand,
was responsible, via Gogol's *Greatcoat*, for the
gallery of the "insulted and injured" in Dostoevsky's novels, from *Poor Folk* onwards. It is known
that the initial idea for his novel *A Raw Youth*
was taken by Dostoevsky from the monologue in
Pushkin's *The Miser Knight*. *The Idiot* was partly
inspired by the *Legend* beginning with the line
"Once there lived a poor knight" which is quoted
in the novel. Also the irrational "Petersburg"

flavour of *The Queen of Spades* left a strong mark in Dostoevsky's novels.

As for Tolstoy, it is enough to quote this extract from a letter addressed to one of his friends on March 30th, 1874, i.e. at the time he was working upon *Anna Karenina*: "You will hardly believe me when I tell you that I have been reading, these last few days since you left, *Tales of Belkin* for the seventh time, and with an enthusiasm I have not felt for a long while. Any author should study this treasure without ceasing. This re-reading has affected me greatly." Tolstoy's literary reaction to *The Prisoner in the Caucasus* has already been mentioned in connection with his novel *The Cossacks*. But, however much Tolstoy tried to debunk the romantic side of the Caucasus, the Rousseauesque going "back to nature" as shown in Aleko (*The Gipsies*) became one of his strongest impulses, until it turned in him, too, as in Aleko, into a blind hatred of all civilisation.

Pictures of Russian country life, such as those in *Onegin*, were continued, and on a broad scale, by Turgenev, Goncharov, Tolstoy and scores of others. Turgenev was a past-master at depicting the autumnal moods of the decaying gentry. Goncharov found his proper medium in characteristic small touches, in *Kleinmalerei*; whereas Tolstoy preferred a full-blooded realism tempered by psychological analysis. As for the "Russian house's annals" type of narrative, it came into its own in Sergey Aksakov's *Family Chronicle*, partly in Tolstoy's *War and Peace*, and in *Anna Karenina*. The first incentive to write *Anna Karenina* was actually due to one of Pushkin's fragments in prose, opening with the sentence "The guests were arriving at the country-house." And Anna herself is supposed to be a portrait of Pushkin's beautiful but unhappy daughter Baroness Hartung.

IV

A special mention should be made of the thematic importance of Pushkin's works, beginning with *Evgeny Onegin*. The Tatyana-Onegin motive (the meeting of a strong woman with a weak "superfluous" man) set an indelible stamp upon the whole of Russian fiction after Pushkin. It is particularly conspicuous in Turgenev's *Rudin* and in Goncharov's *Oblomov* as well as in his *Precipice*. Vera and Marfinka in *The Precipice* represent a carefully worked out analogy between Tatyana and Olga in *Onegin*. Irina, the heroine of Turgenev's *Smoke*, can be defined as an up-to-date Tatyana who first surrenders to the man she once loved but eventually returns to her world of "society." Even Tolstoy's *Anna Karenina* in some respects is less remote from Tatyana than one might think, although she represents at the same time a case of influence through contrast. She too, like Pushkin's heroine, was married to an elderly dignitary, while loving another man after her own heart. But unlike Tatyana she yielded to the voice of her love, after which the moralist Tolstoy summoned all the power of his genius in order to punish her, or rather to make her punish herself, for her "sin."

An unheroic hero, an unexciting and somewhat loose plot, and especially an inconclusive ending, typical of *Onegin*, became adopted almost as a canon by Russian authors whose distaste for the escapist romance (with wedding bells and other blessings at the end) was notorious. Also personal digressions, so frequent in Pushkin's works, penetrated to some extent into Russian fiction, to begin with Gogol's *Dead Souls* (1842), the idea for which had been suggested by Pushkin himself.

But while speaking of the thematic importance of Pushkin's works we cannot possibly by-pass his *History of the Village Goryukhino*. The influence of this fragment was quite out of proportion to its size, especially from the 'forties onwards, when the realism of the "natural school" with its indictments was in the ascendant. The bugbear was of course serfdom. And the author who never tired of attacking it, as well as the other evils of Russian life, was M. Saltykov-Shchedrin (1826–89). He is known outside Russia through his powerful but gloomy novel *The Golovlyov Family*, in which he depicts the disintegration of a decayed family of gentry on the eve of, and after, the abolition of serfdom in 1861. But whereas Pushkin's satire on serfdom is balanced by his sense of humour, in Saltykov-Shchedrin the satirical trend often grows at the expense of humour. His laughter is akin to Gogol's "laughter through tears," with a rancorous *timbre* in it. His stature in literature would be greater had he not mixed his otherwise powerful talent with too much journalism and vitriolic pamphleteering.

Among the characters who took root in Russian realism, the figure of Belkin ought to be pointed out as a product of the Russian sense of humour. Quite in contrast to some foreign opinions, the Russians, like the English, have a strong sense of humour, and, in spite of their seriousness in serious matters, they know how to laugh with relish. History and conditions of life have provided them with much material for that satirical laughter which found an expression in Gogol. But alongside Gogol's satire we also have the magnificent humour of Pushkin. Humour, whether English or Russian, is essentially kindly to its victim. But whereas an Englishman prefers understatement, i.e. a non-committal, impersonal attitude even in his humorous kindness, a Russian enjoys a mixture of comic banter with a note of personal affection and pity. This is why he likes characters who are pathetic and comic in one, like Pushkin's Belkin and his literary progeny. The climax of this pathetic comicality was reached by Dostoevsky in the figure of Stepan Trofimovich in *The Possessed*.

V

Less pronounced was Pushkin's influence upon the development of Russian drama. His *Boris Godunov*, from which he expected a reform of the theatre, not only had to wait six years for permission to be published but was at first considered unsuitable for the stage. True enough, by putting an end to pseudo-classic plays in Russian literature *Boris Godunov* helped to clear the ground for realism on the stage, but the latter received a stronger impetus from Gogol's satirical comedy of manners *The Inspector General* (1836).[1] The man who emulated Pushkin's chronicle-play was the greatest Russian dramatist Alexander Ostrovsky (1823–86). But Ostrovsky took this up more as a side-line, and it cannot be compared with his successful realistic plays dealing with the old-fashioned merchant-class he knew so well. The direct influence of Pushkin the playwright is however in evidence in the dramatic work of Alexey K. Tolstoy (1817–75). His well-known trilogy of historical plays in blank verse, *The Death of Ivan the Terrible*, *Fyodor Ioanych* (*Tsar Theodore*) and *Tsar Boris*, continues in the direction indicated by *Boris Godunov* and actually deals with the same period of "troubles." A. K. Tolstoy paints on a broader canvas than Pushkin, but—unlike Pushkin—he cannot resist the temptation

---

[1] The plot of this comedy, like that of *Dead Souls*, was suggested to Gogol by Pushkin.

to indulge in external operatic effects. In his concern to lay emphasis on the historical personages rather than on the true colour of the epoch in question, and also in his moralising propensity, he is nearer to Schiller than to Pushkin.

On the other hand, Pushkin's work as a whole came to dominate the Russian stage through music, since there is hardly a Russian composer of note who has not found at least some inspiration in Pushkin. This refers not only to his lyrics but to all his works, most of which provided suitable material for operas and ballets. Glinka in 1837–42 turned *Ruslan and Ludmila* into an operatic masterpiece which laid the foundation of Russian national opera. His younger contemporary, Dargomyzhsky, wrote an opera to the text of *Rusalka* (1855) and another, unfinished, to *The Stone Guest*.[1] Tchaikovsky's opera *Evgeny Onegin* (1879) has been on the principal stages all the world over. So has his second well-known opera *The Queen of Spades*. Less known is his *Mazepa*, based on Pushkin's *Poltava*. Musorgsky was responsible for *Boris Godunov* (1870, first produced in 1874), surely one of the greatest of all operas. *Mozart and Salieri*, *The Tale of Tsar Saltan* and *The Golden Cockerel* were turned into operas by Rimsky-Korsakov. Arensky made *Egyptian Nights* into a successful ballet, whereas César Cui (a member of the "big five") composed three operas on

---

[1] Incidentally, Dargomyzhsky's *Rusalka* was produced in London in 1860.

Pushkin's themes: *A Prisoner in the Caucasus*, *A Feast at the Time of Plague* and *A Captain's Daughter*. Two other operas, *Aleko*, based on *The Gipsies*, and *The Miser Knight*, are to the credit of Rakhmaninov. *Snowstorm*, from the *Tales of Belkin*, is the title of an opera by A. S. Taneyev. Another of those five tales, *The Peasant-Lady*, served Glazunov as material for a ballet, while *Dubrovsky* was used for an opera by E. Napravnik.

Among the more recent musical compositions inspired by Pushkin's works the following can be mentioned: *Mavra* (*The Little House in Kolomna*) by Igor Stravinsky; *The Post-Stage Master* by V. Kryukov; *The Tale of the Fisherman and the Fish* by L. Polovinkin; and two ballets—*The Fountain of Bakhchisaray* and *The Prisoner in the Caucasus*—by B. Asafyev. There are also a few foreign composers who borrowed the subject-matter for their operas from Pushkin. Halévy's *The Queen of Spades* is an instance. Another is *Maria Potocka* (based on *The Fountain of Bakhchisaray*) by the Czech composer L. Mekura. Nor should we forget that Mérimée, the author of the story which provided the libretto for Bizet's famous opera, was himself an admirer and translator of Pushkin, whose *Gipsies* actually left some traces in *Carmen*.

All this is only a further proof that Pushkin can be looked upon not only as a great poet and author but also as one of those cultural forces the vitality of which is bound to "live and move eternally," as Belinsky said. It was through him that Russian literature received its focus and at the same time that direction in which the soul of his nation can look for its true image and self-expression. The whole of Russian literature after Pushkin has been above all a process of this kind, and some of its results have been so striking as to astonish the world.

Conclusion

PUSHKIN can be regarded as a cultural complement of Peter the Great. He not only carried the literature of his country to one of its highest summits but also knew how to blend with it the cultural heritage of Europe. Far from clashing with each other, in Pushkin the national and universal elements converged, thus anticipating a synthesis between the two. For this reason it is particularly significant that he became the first important link between the culture of Great Britain and that of Russia. Since the future of the world depends largely on the *rapprochement* between these two countries, it is almost imperative that such a process should first take place in the realm of cultural values. Pushkin was a great pioneer in this respect, and for this reason alone he deserves to be the more widely known in Great Britain.

From a purely Russian point of view, again, it is essential to realise that in addition to being the central figure in Russian literature he also serves as a guarantee of its inner continuity. During the cataclysm of 1917 there were some voices demanding that Pushkin himself should be "thrown overboard" in the name of a proletarian culture, but this tendency was soon overruled.

214

Instead of being relegated to the past, Pushkin became the most cherished cultural possession of the awakened Soviet masses, and this was by no means a small achievement. At the same time, the slogan "Back to Pushkin" was a call to respect the organic continuity of Russian literature and culture in general, regardless of political, social and economic changes. The deeper meaning of this became clear in 1937, when the entire Soviet Union celebrated Pushkin's centenary with an enthusiasm such as could not have been imagined in the old Tsarist Russia. His works are being published in millions of copies. They are being read from the borders of China to those of Afghanistan and India, just as he himself once predicted:

I shall not wholly die! My soul's enchanted music
My ashes will outlive, and know not pale decay;
And famous I shall be while yet a single poet
    Beneath the moon his rhymes shall say.

My verses will be sung throughout all Russia's vastness,
And every race therein the echo will maintain:
Proud grandson of the Slav, and Finn, and yet unfettered
    Tungooze, and Kalmuck on the plain.

For over a hundred years Pushkin's place in the literature of his own country has remained uncontested and unrivalled. The time may come—perhaps it is not far off—when he will also occupy his rightful place in the literature of the world.

215

Bibliography

of Pushkin's works in recent English translations

The Works of Alexander Pushkin, selected and edited, with an introduction, by Avram Yarmolinsky. Translated by Babette Deutsch, T. Keane, Natalia Duddington and others. (Random House, N.Y.; Nonesuch Press, London.)

Pushkin's Poems, a selection translated by Walter Morison, with an introduction by Janko Lavrin. 1945. (Allen & Unwin for Prague Press.)

A Book of Russian Verse, edited, with an introduction by C. M. Bowra. 1943. (Macmillan.)

Poems from the Russian, chosen and translated by Frances C. Cornford and Salaman. 1943. (Faber.)

Verse from Pushkin and Others (containing the *Skazki* and *The Bronze Horseman*), translated by Oliver Elton. (Arnold.)

Six Poems from Pushkin (it includes *Ruslan and Ludmila, Poltava, The Prisoner of the Caucasus*), translated by Jacob Krup. 1936. (The Galleon Press, N.Y.)

The Russian Wonderland (*Coq d'Or, The Tale of the Fisherman and the Fish, Czar Saltan*) translated by Boris Brasol. 1936. (Paiseley Press, N.Y.)

Evgeny Onegin, translated by Oliver Elton, with a foreword by Desmond MacCarthy and illustrated by M. V. Dobujinsky. 1943. (Pushkin Press.)

Eugene Onegin, translated by Dorothea Prall Radin and George Z. Patrick. 1937. (University of California Press.)

Another translation of *Onegin*, done by Babette Deutsch, is included in the above-mentioned *The Works of Alexander Pushkin*, edited by Avram Yarmolinsky.

216

Boris Godunov, translated by A. Hayes. 1919. (Kegan Paul.)

Little Tragedies, translated by V. de S. Pinto and W. H. Marshall, with an introduction by Janko Lavrin. (The New Europe Publishing Company.) 1946.

The Captain's Daughter, and Other Tales, translated, with an introduction, by Natalie Duddington. 1933. (Everyman's Library.)

Works on Pushkin in English

Pushkin, by Prince D. S. Mirsky. 1926. (Routledge.)

Pushkin, by Ernest J. Simmons. 1937. (Harvard University Press; Oxford University Press.)

Alexander Pushkin, by S. H. Cross and Ernest Simmons. 1937. (American Institute for Cultural Relations with Soviet Union.)

Centenary Essays for Pushkin, by S. H. Cross and E. J. Simmons. 1937. (Harvard University Press.)

Prelude to Parnassus, by James Cleugh. 1936. (Barker.)

The Mighty Three (with an essay on Pushkin), by Boris Brasol. 1934. (Payson, N.Y.)

A short but excellent chapter on Pushkin is to be found in *Russian Literature*, by Maurice Baring (Home University Library); also in *A History of Russian Literature*, by Prince D. S. Mirsky. (Routledge.)

Index of Names

INDEX OF NAMES

INDEX OF NAMES

INDEX OF NAMES

223